Chicago's Famous Buildings

a photographic guide
to the city's architectural landmarks
and other notable buildings

Chicago's Famous Buildings

second edition
revised and enlarged

edited by Arthur Siegel
descriptive text by J. Carson Webster

with contributions by
Carl W. Condit   Hugh Dalziel Duncan
Wilbert R. Hasbrouck

The University of Chicago Press
Chicago & London

The University of Chicago Press, Chicago 60637
The University of Chicago Press, Ltd., London

International Standard Book Number: 0-226-75685-8
Library of Congress Catalog Card Number: 69-15367

Publication of this book was made possible
by generous grants from the Graham Foundation
for Advanced Studies in the Fine Arts
and from the City of Chicago

Contents

Foreword to Second Edition

It is always a pleasant task to report a successful venture; and so it is in the case of the first edition of *Chicago's Famous Buildings*. The excellent public response more than justified the faith of the City of Chicago and the Graham Foundation in this venture. We now feel certain that our decision to proceed with this revised edition is both proper and propitious. This new edition has been extensively revised, including the addition of several new buildings, constructed during the past four years.

Once again, we are grateful to the Graham Foundation and its president, Charles F. Murphy, Sr., and to the City of Chicago and Mayor Richard J. Daley for their generosity in providing the necessary funds to publish this revised edition.

As to the Commission on Chicago Architectural Landmarks, it too has been reorganized and revised and has been renamed, the Commission on Chicago Historical and Architectural Landmarks. An ordinance adopted by the Chicago City Council in April 1968, provides for an expansion of the powers and responsibilities of the Commission. The members of the new commission are delighted to sponsor this second edition.

IRA J. BACH
Secretary, Commission on Chicago
Historical and Architectural Landmarks

Foreword to First Edition

The Chicago School of Architecture is famous the world over, but visitors seeking out its best works have sometimes had difficulty locating them. Indeed, the people who live here have often been unaware of or unable to find the structures for which their city is so widely known. So the need for this book has been clear for some time.

In 1957 Mayor Richard J. Daley emphasized the need for preserving Chicago's architectural heritage by documentation and citation as well as actual preservation. He therefore recommended to the Chicago City Council that a commission be created to designate certain buildings as architectural landmarks. On the basis of an ordinance drafted by Alderman Leon Despres the Commission on Architectural Landmarks was organized, with seven members appointed by the Mayor and Daniel Canton Rich, then director of the Art Institute, as first chairman.

A committee of prominent architects and art historians was chosen to advise the Commission. After visiting many buildings that had been proposed as landmarks and after much deliberation, the Commission finally selected thirty-nine structures which met the criteria developed by the advisory committee and approved by the Commission. In a public ceremony Mayor Daley presented to the building owners distinctive plaques identifying the structures as architectural landmarks of Chicago. This means they are also to be considered landmarks in the history of modern architecture, for they constitute the most important innovations in the art of building since the Gothic cathedrals.

The ordinance creating the Commission directed that it "list and identify Chicago's architectural landmarks . . . [and] take steps to stimulate public interest in the identification and preservation of such landmarks." This directive made preparation of a guidebook an early project of the Commission.

The Commission solicited and received financial assistance from the Graham Foundation for Advanced Studies in the Fine Arts. A matching sum was received from the City of Chicago by action of the City Council upon recommendation of Mayor Daley.

Both the Commission and the Graham Foundation immediately agreed to expand the publication to include additional buildings. The advisory committee of the Commission was caled in to serve once more and responded by recommending many more worthy buildings, some on the basis of architectural merit; others because they are considered to have a special symbolic, sentimental, or historic importance; a few for reasons of general interest. Meanwhile, Illinois Institute of Technology architectural students, under the direction of Dean George Danforth, measured and prepared plans of the architectural landmarks. Photography students of the Institute of Design of the Illinois Institute of Technology helped in photographing many of the buildings. The architectural firm of Skidmore, Owings and Merrill prepared the excellent maps. Arthur Siegel, who had already been responsible for supervising the photographic work by students and others, was appointed editor, and with his dedicated direction this book has been brought into final form.

Grateful thanks are due Mayor Richard J. Daley for his splendid co-operation with the Commission. His pride in Chicago and his appreciation for its exciting architectural history have been an inspiration.

The generosity of the Graham Foundation and its president, Charles F. Murphy, made the production of this guidebook possible. We are also grateful to John Entenza, director of the Foundation, for his professional assistance.

Commission Vice-Chairman Samuel A. Lichtmann headed the advisory committee and the guidebook committee. Our gratitude is offered to him and to his committees, as it is to Judge Augustine Bowe, who is Chairman of the Commission on Chicago Architectural Landmarks. Our thanks for the concise bibliography go to Miss Ruth Schoneman of the Burnham Library.

It is hoped that *Chicago's Famous Buildings* will assist not only the tourist to Chicago but also its citizens who take pride in their architectural heritage. It is hoped also that architects, engineers, planners, and students will use this book as a reference and for inspiration in their work.

IRA J. BACH

Publisher's Preface

Publication of the original edition of *Chicago's Famous Buildings* in 1965, coincided happily with one of the major building booms in the history of the city—a boom which quickly proved to be, in part, a revival of the Chicago School of Architecture. The quick success of the Guide was thus accompanied by developments bound to date it more rapidly than had been anticipated. We are grateful that renewed financial support from the City of Chicago and the Graham Foundation for Advanced Study in the Fine Arts has helped us in bringing out, only four years after the first publication, a revised and augmented second edition of *Chicago's Famous Buildings*.

The second edition has benefited from the talents of John Massey, who has redesigned the work page by page. This has made it possible to group the different categories of buildings in a more convenient sequence from the point of view of either the sightseer or the professional student of architecture.

A number of new buildings, among them some which have been recognized at once as major masterpieces of contemporary architecture, were erected since the publication of the first edition. They have been included in the second edition, in part replacing older buildings which were demolished in that same period. Text and photographs of the newly included buildings within the city limits were prepared by Professor Carl Condit of Northwestern University. They are: numbers 25, 26, 80, 81, 84, 85, 89, 92, 93, 104, 105, 106, 107, 108, 109, 110, 111, and 112. In addition, a section on the Prairie School has been added. Although the Guide was originally limited to the city's legal limits, it seemed anomalous to publish a work entitled *Chicago's Famous Buildings,* which did not include a fair showing of the suburban domestic buildings of Frank Lloyd Wright and his followers.

This necessitated the assembly of a new section of the Guide, for which descriptive text, photographs, and a map were supplied by Mr. Wilbert Hasbrouck, Executive Director, Chicago Chapter, American Institute of Architects.

All the other descriptive texts accompanying the photographs are the work of J. Carson Webster of Northwestern University. They were prepared by Professor Webster for the first edition, and are reprinted exactly as written by him except for certain minor corrections which he has supplied.

The maps for this edition were provided by the Center for Urban Studies, Chicago, Illinois.

Chicago's Famous Buildings

The Chicago School: Principles . . .

Hugh Dalziel Duncan

The buildings illustrated in this guide are part
of the great cultural heritage of America.
Chicago is the national, and indeed the world,
capital for historical landmarks of modern
architecture. Almost the whole history of what
we call "contemporary design" can be
examined in Chicago. For Chicago is the
birthplace of modern architecture, and some
of the buildings illustrated here are among the
first, and greatest, examples of it. That is why
architects come from all over the world to
study these great buildings. Chicago is the
urban center of the life and work of Frank
Lloyd Wright and Mies van der Rohe, who,
along with Le Corbusier, are the great
architects of our time. Another Chicagoan,
Louis Henri Sullivan, was the master from
whom Wright, Mies, and Le Corbusier drew
inspiration in developing their talents and
their understanding of the architect's role in
society.

The architecture of the Chicago School was
first considered a style among many styles.
From 1890 until about 1920, it was thought of
as commercial or industrial architecture. In
the twenties, many critics dismissed the work
of the Chicago School as representing a crude
"commercial" style to be "refined" by other
architects. Such architects, mostly classicists,
were educated in European schools and
worked with clients who were interested in
beautiful buildings so long as the beauty was
European, not American. Sullivan, it was
admitted, had done some good ornament,
but this was really wasted, and even "out of
place," on commercial buildings. But in the
thirties, as the work of Le Corbusier and Perret
in France, Behrens, Gropius, Mendelsohn, and
Mies van der Rohe in Germany, Berlage and

Dudok in Holland, and Frank Lloyd Wright in America began to be accepted as genuinely creative, even conventional critics were forced to admit that modern architecture might be more than a passing fad.

An order of architecture, unlike a style, expresses a way of life. It is the expression of the community, not simply that of a class or an individual. This community for Jenney, Adler, Root, Burnham, and Wright was the democratic community. For however the architects of the Chicago School differed on design and however they argued about the relationship of engineering and architecture, they all agreed that the only architecture worth having was a democratic architecture. Indeed, Sullivan taught that democracy *depended* on its architects as much as on its statesmen or businessmen. He argued, with deep and prophetic conviction, that until democracy produced a good architecture and good art, it could not produce a good life for its citizens. Thus from the very beginning modern architecture in Chicago was part of a search for a social philosophy of democracy, as well as a search for perfection of form.

But while it was easy enough to talk about a people's art and a democratic architecture, it was another matter to produce it. In both his buildings and his early talks to Chicagoans on architecture, Sullivan asked questions: What is the proper form for a democratic architecture, and what kinds of human relationships will be possible in this new architecture? He answered the first by proposing that whatever the use of a building, its form must follow its function—not a mechanical function, like a traffic flow, circulation of air, heating, lighting, etc., but *human* function. He thought that the architect must ask himself: How can I enhance the human satisfaction of acting wtihin my building or the communities I design? If I design a house of prayer, how do I make prayer more significant? If I design a department store, how do I make shopping more pleasurable? If I design a factory, how do I make work healthy and pleasurable? If I design a tomb, how do I make the sorrowing family feel the serenity and peace of death as a memory of life?

This is what Sullivan meant by his constantly repeated phrase: "A building is an act." And it is also what he meant by insisting that a building, indeed all architecture, is a moral act because it is an aesthetic act. In his *Kindergarten Chats,* the record of the spiritual voyage of a young architect, Sullivan takes us on a walk through the streets of Chicago, his city of joy and sorrow. As we walk beside the master we discover that he reads buildings as we read character in the faces of people. Perhaps this is why he hated "phony" buildings. He thought a bank should look like a friendly meeting place for neighbors who had come to see each other and to talk over their problems with bank officials. A bank which looked like a fort, a great vault, a Roman temple, or a Gothic cathedral, enraged him. Why, he asked, does the banker not dress in a Roman toga and talk in Latin? And why, he asked over and over again, is the banker ashamed to be an American in his expression of a most characteristic American act—the exchange of money?

Nor would Sullivan agree to any hierarchy of content, or to the commonly accepted distinction between fine and applied art. Like Thorstein Veblen and Frank Lloyd Wright, who followed Sullivan's teaching, he argued that invention was the mother of necessity. What the engineer invented, or the artist created, became needs. That is, the people did not have needs which they "asked" the artist to satisfy, nor were there "social forces," like evolution or the class struggle, which determined the forms of architecture. The people and the artist *shared* problems. The true democratic artist accepted these problems as his problems, and tried to solve them through the creation of buildings and cities which would enhance the democratic qualities of human relationships. The democratic architect must create communities where *all* men could walk in dignity, freedom, and joy in human brotherhood.

Thus, in the development of the Burnham Plan for the city of Chicago, the problem of traffic, of the city as a community in motion, was faced in common by architects, engineers, sociologists, economists, civic officials, and representatives of the people. The art involved in the creation of such a plan was certainly applied art, but it never occurred to Burnham that he should not use all the resources of fine art to create his plan. True, the purpose of any city plan was to insure a good flow of traffic, but Chicagoans did not want their traffic to flow right through or around the city. They wanted to make it easy for people to get in and out of the Loop, but they also wanted people to stop in their hotels, stores, and restaurants, and to find homes in the city. Burnham, Root, Sullivan, and Wright argued that people would stop only if the Loop, and the whole of the city, were interesting and beautiful. The first mark of beauty in architecture was the way in which it brought order into the human environment. A city was beautiful because it solved the problem (among others) of how to get automobiles and people through its streets, house and feed them during their stay in the city, and offer fit dwelling places for families.

Sullivan, and certainly Sullivan's great pupil, Wright, were as sensitive as Burnham to the need for planning. Wright warned Chicagoans at the time the original Chicago Plan was promoted that the future of our city would be a race between the elevator and the automobile, and he declared that wise Chicagoans would bet on the automobile. But Root, Sullivan, and Wright were more concerned than Burnham with the kinds of human satisfactions achitecture could give people, the humble as well as the great, in their daily personal lives. They asked State Street merchants: What is the use of bringing people to the Loop unless our stores are exciting, our factories decent places to work, our hotels comfortable and luxurious, and our city a suitable environment for families?

Questions like these had been asked before,

but few architects had asked them in relation to *all* the people of a community—a community where hundreds of thousands of people and millions of tons of goods must be moved with every turn of the clock. The great cities of the past, such as Rome, were planned for movement and the sheltering of huge crowds for special civic events, but never before in the history of the world had there been need to design for the swift movement of machines as well as people. And never before was a city designed by architects who asked themselves: How can I design for the greatest number of people and yet give each individual the greatest possible satisfaction? Thus, when Adler designed his great Auditorium, he approached acoustics as the art of distributing sound to the largest possible audience. He wanted the poorest student in the most remote section of the Auditorium, as well as the rich and mighty in their boxes, to hear. In hall after hall he tried to bring sound, in all its purity and beauty, to the people. His successes in the Auditorium and Carnegie Hall are now part of our national heritage.

In the same spirit, Sullivan designed the Schlesinger and Mayer Store (now the Carson Pirie Scott Store). Like the owners, he was eager to attract the largest number of people into the store, but, unlike the bankers and their architects, he did not want to attract customers through inspiring them with awe. He wanted to make shopping a joyful, exciting event, not for just a few rich customers, but for all the people. Nor did he think of the store as an imposing facade which could be used to lure people inside. Without and within it was to be a great bazaar whose tone of elegance, gaiety, and graciousness would give women of all ranks pleasure in their femininity and create a gracious stage for the spending of money in a tasteful and dignified manner.

Sullivan did not think of the Schlesinger and Mayer Store as a proud, soaring tower, thrusting up into the sky. He had designed and built such towers. But a store for women should not be a proud, arrogant tower. So he accentuated the horizontal plane, the human plane of man on earth, which Wright and Jensen used so often in their homes for Chicago families. Shopping should be gay and festive, the trip downtown a small adventure, and for women who were just beginning to appear in public without their men, stores must be a gracious retreat from the burly masculine tone of the street or the wholesale store which merely tolerated retail customers. Each floor must be a great but elegant stage filled with treasures from the four corners of the earth. Onto this stage timid young immigrant women, middle-class wives seeking good buys, and the stately matrons of high society were invited. The floors of these great State Street stores became a great promenade, like the square of an ancient city, where all came to see—and to be seen. Here, for the first time, the "shawl trade" and the "carriage trade" met as audiences before each other.

The public schools designed by Dwight H. Perkins show this same spirit in education. Carl Schurz High School and Grover Cleveland Elementary School were designed to create a beautiful and serene experience for children and youths of all classes and races. They were in every sense people's schools. The sons and daughters of poor immigrants who went through these schools have told us what it meant to go from the squalor of poverty and ignorance to such buildings. For many, the hours spent in the school were their only experience of a decent habitation. As such students walked through the doors of these schools, the promise of democracy became real. In their public, if not in their private, lives, they could walk the earth with dignity as sons and daughters of a city whose civic leaders believed that *all* men should be decently clothed, housed, fed, and educated.

And nowhere does the profundity of the work of the Chicago School show more clearly than in Sullivan's Getty Tomb in Graceland Cemetery. In some ways this tomb, which Frank Lloyd Wright cherished so deeply, is Chicago's most profound utterance in democratic art. Beside the grandiose mausoleums of Chicago's great families from 1875 to 1910, the Carrie Eliza Getty Tomb stands in quiet simplicity. As Hugh Morrison says in his book *Louis Sullivan: Prophet of Modern Architecture:* "The sentiment expressed in the majority of monuments is the preoccupation with death, its awfulness, its inevitability, its utter permanence. . . . A different spirit animates Sullivan's tombs. They celebrate, not the permanence of death, but the permanence of life; they express in terms of lyric beauty that a man or woman has *lived,* not merely he or she has died." This is expressed, not in gold or marble, but in blocks of gray Bedford limestone whose rich ornament is subordinated to architectural expression.

Outside of Chicago, few understood the significance of Chicago design. Adams, Norton, Bourget, and other visitors, during the years following World's Columbian Exposition of 1893, told their readers and hearers that Chicago architecture, as indeed the whole city, was based on making money. And since the making of money, if not its possession, was, in the eyes of traditional aesthetes and the aristocracies of Europe and America, essentially an ignoble pursuit, how could culture, to say nothing of great art, come from business people? Easterners like Adams, Norton, Henry James, and Edith Wharton admitted that Chicago was "interesting" and even "significant," but its significance as a center of American art was simply beyond their comprehension. Their prejudice against business and their fear of the "alien" people pouring into American cities made it impossible for them to consider the relationships between money and art in anything but negative terms.

Such considerations are still difficult for many critics, professors, and historians. Yet, if we are asked to make any sense out of what happened in Chicago and to think at all about why it produced the greatest architecture of our time, we must accept the fact that the greatest clients of Chicago architects were businessmen and their wives. Even

Henry-Russell Hitchcock, whose *Architecture: Nineteenth and Twentieth Centuries* is the standard history of modern architecture, is obviously puzzled by how Chicago with "no established traditions, no real professional leaders, and ignorance of the architectural styles, past or present" produced the great architecture of our time—an architecture which owes its existence to "enlightened commercial patrons" who "demanded and often received the best architecture of their day." He is careful to make the point that it is a mistake to disregard the architectural genius of Chicago where the "strictly *architectural,* as well as the technical and social, significance of the major commercial monuments of the nineteenth century will be evident."

The contributions of Chicago engineers to the building art, to the creation of the city, and finally to the great Chicago Plan have often been told. Jenney's Home Insurance Building contained the first iron frame—the precursor of the steel cage. It was the first building whose walls were not load-bearing. But before the tall buildings could be built, foundations strong enough to carry their great weight in swampy soil had to be developed. Many new types of foundations were invented. Indeed, Chicago engineers were so advanced that the architects themselves were not able to keep up with them. Chicago grain elevators, which were built in the seventies on the banks of the River, used piling for foundations. Yet it was not until after 1890 that architects made common use of this type of foundation.

The new buildings of Chicago were not constructed by the city, by religious organizations, by educational institutions, or by private groups as palatial edifices. They were built by businessmen and they were built for profit. Even the Auditorium, which was the civic and cultural center of Chicago for many years, was built to make money. It was a civic center, a hotel, and an office building. It was financed like any other business venture on the expectation of profit. George H. Pullman built what he hoped would be a worker's utopia, but he made clear from the very start that, unlike the older American utopias founded by religious and cooperative groups, his utopia was strictly a business venture. The town of Pullman would prove that workers could be decently housed, fed, clothed, educated, entertained, and even worship God, at a profit to those who would build communities for them.

The women of Chicago, too, were as radical as their men—indeed, in some ways more radical. They wanted to lead public as well as private lives, and they wanted to lead simple and informal lives within the home. They wanted to be what they called "neighborly." The houses Root, and later Wright, built for them were built on "lots." These houses, unlike those in older cities, never abandoned the earlier spirit of Chicago, which, in its early days before the Fire, was known as the Garden City because of its many yards with gardens and because the number of trees which sheltered the simple one-story "cottages" built by carpenters after the elaborate Greek Revival homes of Latrobe. Chicago women did not want homes surrounded by walls, but with porches and large bay windows, open to all four sides of the yard, and close enough to the street to return greetings from neighbors. In a sense, they wanted to live in 1880 as most suburban families want to live now in the 1960's. As early as 1874 Chicagoans were boasting of their suburbs and, a few years later, of their parks along the lake front, on the West Side, and in the forest preserves.

But the achievements of Chicago businessmen, the daring and organizing ability of her builders, and the brilliance of her engineers, great though they were, do not explain the Chicago School of architecture. For the genius of architecture is formed space, and however great the community and however abundant men, money, land, and people may be, they cannot produce a great architecture without the vision and imagination of the architect. When all is said and done, Chicago did not produce great architects because it gave them the opportunity to build a city or to rebuild a city destroyed by fire. Boston and San Francisco suffered from great fires. New York, in common with many other American cities, increased rapidly in size and population. Yet Chicago, and Chicago alone, from 1875 into the 1960's, has turned to great architects for her city plan, for her buildings, for her schools, and for her homes.

This happened because of the genius of Louis H. Sullivan, who struggled through his fifty-one years of practice in Chicago (1873–1924) to create in his buildings and to communicate in his writing an aesthetic of democratic architecture. This became known as "functionalism." The spirit of functional form was the expression of the social purpose of the building in its structure. Sullivan taught that each building must be unique. He never repeated his ornament. Each building had a "spirit" which must be respected. The expression of this spirit was as much a part of its "utility" as the plumbing. For only when the building *evoked* human satisfactions determined by the form itself could it become architecture. And only when such form could be reduced to some kind of principle could it become an order, and not merely a style, of architecture.

Architectural principles are reached, as Sullivan, Root, Wright, and Mies van der Rohe taught, by asking: What is the chief characteristic of the structure? To answer this for the tall building, Sullivan said that the chief characteristic of the tall office building was its loftiness. This "is the very organ-tone of its appeal. It must be in turn dominant chord in the [architect's] expression of it, the true excitant of his imagination. It must be tall, every inch of it tall. The force and power of altitude must be in it, the glory and pride of exaltation must be in it. It must be every inch a proud and soaring thing, rising in sheer exaltation that from bottom to top it is a unit without a single dissenting line. . . ."

The deeper principle underlying the character of the soaring tower is that the outward expression, structure, "design or whatever we may choose [to call it], of the tall office building should in the very nature of things follow the functions of the building. . . ." Architectural art has failed thus far, Sullivan taught, because it has not yet found a way to become truly plastic: "It does not yield to the poet's touch." It is the only art "for which the multitudinous rhythms of outward nature, the manifold fluctuations of man's inner being have no significance, no place." Greek architecture, great as it was, lacked rhythm because it was not related to nature, and because the great art of music had not been born. While possessing serenity, "it lacked the divinely human element of mobility." Gothic architecture, "with sombre ecstatic eye," evoked a copious and rich variety of expression, but it "lacked the unitary comprehension, the absolute consciousness and mastery of pure form that can come alone of unclouded and serene contemplation, of perfect repose and peace of mind."

Thus, while the Greek knew the "statics, the Goth the dynamics," of architecture, neither of them suspected the mobile equilibrium of it, because neither of them "divined the movement and stability of nature."

Failing in this, both have fallen short, "and must pass away when the true, the *Poetic Architecture* shall arise—that architecture which shall speak with clearness, with eloquence, and with warmth, of the fullness, the completeness of man's intercourse with nature and with his fellow men." The search for a new kind of movement in architecture, which Sullivan called "mobile equilibrium," is the clue to the aesthetics of the Chicago School of the past, as it is to Mies van der Rohe's work in the present.

When we look at Chicago's towers, we sense at once the tension between horizontal and vertical thrust. The resolution of this tension creates a "mobile equilibrium." As our eye travels up the massive flanks of the Monadnock, along the glass bays of the Reliance, the steel piers of 860–80 Lake Shore

Drive, or the Inland Steel Company Building, we experience at once the soaring quality of the great tower. We are freed from earth and carried up into the sky. We are no longer earthbound: a new kind of power fills our being as a sense of movement—movement into the sky—sweeps over us. But the eye also rests on horizontal planes whose intersection with the vertical thrust arrests the eyes long enough to make our upward flight a rhythmic progression, not a headlong rush into space. The horizontal plane acts like a musical phrase.

Sometimes the spirit of form is horizontal; at other times it is vertical. Carson Pirie Scott, the Robie House, the Illinois Institute of Technology Campus, accentuate horizontal planes. For Sullivan, Wright, and Jens Jensen, the great landscape architect, the horizontal line was the prairie line, the great rolling prairie of the Middle West which moved our artists so deeply. Wright, speaking for every middle western artist, said: "I loved the prairie by instinct as, itself, a great simplicity; the trees, the flowers, and sky were thrilling by contrast . . . the plan . . . serene beneath a wonderful sweep of sky." The horizontal plane becomes one of movement, flow, and continuity. And it is the human plane, the plane along which man walks with other men. The vertical thrust gives us a sense of power, but the horizontal brings us serenity and peace.

And this, in the last analysis, is the power of these great Chicago buildings. They are a humane expression of a new way of life—the modern urban community based on money and technology. They are humane because the architects of the Chicago School, from the first generation of the seventies and eighties to the third generation of the sixties in our century, have followed the teachings of their master, Sullivan. "With me," he said, "architecture is not an art, but a religion, and that religion but a part of democracy." In this spirit our best buildings and communities have been—and will be—designed. The love of the common man has been the glory of Chicago. The belief that only when he is decently housed can democracy survive has been the moral glory of our architecture. The conviction that he must be beautifully housed and sheltered has become the aesthetic credo of modern architecture. Who is to do this—the state, the businessman, or the powerful institutions of the democratic community itself —is by no means certain. But that it *must* be done is certain. For democracy cannot exist without good architecture, and good architecture in turn can be created only among men who walk the earth in freedom and dignity.

The Chicago School: . . . and Practice

Carl W. Condit

In the chaos of architectural styles that prevails today, Chicago has reasserted its great building tradition in a body of work that may be traced directly back to the days when the city launched the modern movement in architecture and structural techniques. The motives behind this contemporary resurgence include negative as well as positive aspects. One is a reaction against the slick and faceless curtain wall of most commercial building, that shallow and often gaudy wrapping that makes us wonder whether architecture is no more than a variation on the art of packaging. On the positive side, the architects are seeking again to exploit the potentially dynamic quality of the structural frame of steel and concrete, and to explore the possibilities of new variations on older framing techniques. Whatever the motive, it is clear that the current work represents a deliberate return to the basic principle of the Chicago School: an aesthetic statement, developed through structure, of the necessary physical character of the building.

. The original Chicago School of architecture, from its inception to its last days, flourished over the half-century that extended from 1875 to 1925. By 1910 the movement had produced an original, indigenous, and organic architecture for every kind of building—office skyscrapers, hotels and apartments, warehouses and factories, residences, schools, and churches. In the extraordinary decades of the eighties and nineties, the architects and engineers of Chicago developed the structural system of the contemporary multistory building and most of the essential forms of modern architecture. "Here is where it all began," as the editors of *Architectural Forum* recently wrote.

From the beginning this movement divided into two major streams whose leading figures were William Le Baron Jenney and Louis H. Sullivan. Jenney was a strict utilitarian, an empiricist who sought the most economical forms of building to satisfy the functional requirements. His aims were maximum efficiency and economy of construction, open interior space, and the maximum admission of natural light. The external form that grew out of this program is distinguished mainly by the articulated or cellular wall of "Chicago windows," a basic rectangular pattern corresponding in its geometry to the underlying frame of iron or steel and surmounting an open base of glass like a continuous transparent screen. Sullivan, on the other hand, was a self-conscious romantic who treated a building as a plastic object molded to give expression to the strong feeling that the new technology aroused in him.

In spite of Jenney's narrow approach, his influence led to a great diversity of forms derived organically from the underlying skeltal structure. It is best revealed by the work of Holabird and Roche, the most prolific of the Chicago architects during the heroic age. Sullivan's work tended to be subjective, somewhat at odds with the impersonal commercial spirit, and his legacy was passed on chiefly to Frank Lloyd Wright, his greatest and most famous protégé.

If we look carefully at a few of the more famous buildings of the original Chicago School, we can readily see in them the spiritual ancestry of the best contemporary designs. The articulated wall of rectangular cells became the primary visual feature of these first representatives of a new architectural style. Even the exposed steelwork of such recent buildings as the Continental Center and the Civic Center was anticipated long ago in the iron spandrel plates in the facade of the old Brunswick (originally Studebaker) Building, designed by Solon S. Beman and erected at 629 South Wabash Avenue in 1895. The same feature appears in the spandrel plates at the first story of Jenney's Sears Roebuck Store, at State and Van Buren streets, and in his Manhattan Building, at 431 South Dearborn Street, both completed by 1891.

Sullivan's Carson Pirie Scott Store, the masterpiece of the Chicago School and America's greatest work of commercial architecture, represents a formal elaboration of the principle of structural form. Here the neutral cage of iron and steel is transformed into fine architecture through Sullivan's unerring sense of proportion, his ornamental skill, and his exact calculation of the depth of the window reveals to give maximum power to the elevation.

The horizontal elongation of wide-bayed framing appears most strikingly in the huge concrete warehouse of Montgomery Ward and Company, designed by Schmidt, Garden and Martin. The architects of this building deliberately intensified the natural horizontality of the long bands of concrete girders. The same motif distinguishes Wright's Robie House, although here it is developed into a complex pattern of intersecting planes. The Carson Store was completed in 1906, the warehouse in 1908. Fifty years later these features of what was once known as the "Chicago style" were again becoming prominent in the city's buildings.

The opening of the masonry bearing wall in a way that anticipates the contemporary load-bearing truss of concrete is most apparent in Burnham and Root's classic Monadnock Building (1889–91), an austere geometric refinement of the rich dress of their earlier Rookery (1885–86). The projecting bay of the Monadnock was first adapted to the multistory commercial block by Holabird and Roche, but it was given its purest expression by Clinton J. Warren in the Congress Hotel. (Warren designed the original north block, completed in 1893, but Holabird and Roche followed his program in the later south wing, opened, as it now is, in 1907.) The Congress, recently renovated, remains one of the finest works of hotel design in the United States.

Europe could offer no parallel to the Chicago movement at its height. When the leading pioneers—Le Corbusier, Gropius, Mies van der Rohe—began to win attention, even their best designs seemed coldly abstract beside the great richness and variety of the Chicago work. In one of the ironies of our cultural history, however, when modern architecture revived in the United States, it did so under the impetus of European importations. It was an old story—the distrust of native achievements, the belief that Europe must always be the fountainhead of new artistic and intellectual creations. The early work of the European pioneers revealed a sure mastery of the new structural techniques and their formal possibilities, but it was a prime misfortune that the so-called International Style should have swept everything else before it.

This state of affairs continued for nearly two decades, from 1930 to 1950, when the modern movement in the United States was rapidly winning its triumph over the eclecticism of the immediate past. The revolutionary structural inventions of our century, especially reinforced concrete shells, plates, and prestressed members, like the new architectural forms, were all of European origin. With the enormous volume of building that came after World War II, the new inventions spread into such a variety of forms that the idea of a consistent style became an anachronism. Indeed, the long-debated questions—what have we accomplished and where are we going?—are more controversial than ever.

The new Chicago School was established primarily by Mies van der Rohe, who has enjoyed an unbroken series of major commissions in the building boom that followed the war. The Promontory Apartments on South Lake Shore Drive near 56th Street (1948–49) is the first of Mies's fourteen apartment towers that stand singly or in groups along the lakeshore or at the west edge of Lincoln Park. Promontory is unique among these internationally celebrated buildings and belongs exactly to the idiom of the Chicago School. It is the first one in which the naked concrete frame provides the dominant features of the elevation. The outermost columns and girders stand out strong and clear, each rectangular bay enframing a sweep of glass surmounting the narrow spandrel of brick.

Promontory was immediately influential in apartment design. Pace Associates carried the principle to its logical ultimate in the apartment building at the southeast corner of Sheridan Road and Oakdale Avenue (1951–52), where the street and rear elevations are reduced to the exposed concrete frame alone, the entire bay being filled with glass. Since then, the articulated wall of exposed framing members, brick spandrels, and glass has appeared in many large apartment projects, most notably the quarter-circular building at 1150 North Lake Shore Drive, designed by Hausner and Macsai, and the Imperial Towers and Sandburg Village of Solomon and Cordwell.

Meanwhile, Mies had turned to steel construction and offered a strikingly different structural form in Crown Hall, built in 1955–56 on the campus of the Illinois Institute of Technology. The building is a single enclosure of glass supported by four welded rigid frames prominently displayed outside the building envelope. The result is a technical and aesthetic masterpiece of pure geometric form.

But Mies preferred the delicate vertical tracery of the later apartments and IIT buildings. The Chicago tradition in its original character passed to the hands of the enormously prolific firm of Skidmore, Owings and Merrill. Their Inland Steel Building, at Monroe and Dearborn streets (1955–57), is a remarkable *tour de force* in the expression of welded steel framing. The 19-story glass prism contains no interior columns, the primary bearing elements being seven pairs of columns located outside the planes of the long elevations. The floors are carried on transverse girders of 58-foot clear span, a characteristic which makes the Inland Steel Building the first of the wide-bayed structures that are now the hallmark of Chicago building. A novel feature in the planning of the Inland is the separation of elevators and utilities into a tower set wholly apart from the rental area of the main block. The entire building volume is thus divided into the "served" and "servant" areas that Louis I. Kahn later made famous in the brick and concrete structure of the Richards Medical Research Laboratory at the University of Pennsylvania.

The Skidmore firm dropped the Miesian tracery of the Inland Steel in favor of unadorned engineering in the Hartford Insurance Building, built in 1960–61 at Wacker Drive and Monroe Streets. If the Inland is the celebration of technique, the Hartford is technique itself. All one sees here are the columns and floor edges of the flat-slab framing, a system of reinforced concrete construction without beams and girders. The building represents the ultimate in purification of the Chicago style, sharpened and intensified by the functional device of setting the window planes well back from the outer edges of the framing members.

The enthusiasm for wide-bayed steel framing gathered momentum. The traditional skeleton was greatly elongated on horizontal planes in the Continental Center, designed by C. F. Murphy Associates and built in 1961–62 at Wabash Avenue and Jackson Boulevard. Another building with a column-free interior, it is square in plan, the 42-foot bays disposed around three sides of a central court enclosing elevators and utilities. The peculiar combination of force and dignity in the elevations of the Continental Center arises from a strictly empirical approach. The depth of girder required by the wide bay immediately raises the question: How can one justify this costly sacrifice of vertical space? It is a case of structure scientifically designed for economy and utility: the girders are deep enough to allow ducts and conduits to pass through them; the large bays reduce the number of columns and hence the expensive foundation and caisson work of the Chicago region; and the deep girders, rigidly fixed to the columns, provide the necessary stability against wind without any other bracing elements.

Certain features of the Continental design are particularly significant for the new aesthetic currents. The naked steelwork of the street elevations is painted a flat black, the perfect antithesis to the glittering package of the advertisers and its equivalent in most contemporary architecture. The floors and partitions of the lobby are unpolished granite, hard, rough-textured, and durable, suggesting a deliberate choice of surface harshness.

C. F. Murphy Associates, chief architects, with Skidmore, Owings and Merrill, and Loebl, Schlossman and Bennett as associated architects, carried the principle of wide-bayed framing to a climax in their staggering design for Chicago's new Civic Center, under construction since 1963 on the block bounded by Dearborn, Washington, Clark and Randolph streets. The 648-foot tower—the highest in Chicago at the time of its completion—will be carried on 16 massive primary columns set for a maximum span of 87 feet. This unprecedented spacing requires an underfloor system of beams in the form of trusses with a uniform depth of 5 feet 6 inches. The depth of the floor trusses was calculated for the load on the maximum span but held uniform for shorter spans again to allow the passage of ducts and conduits through the floor framing. The huge members of the steel skeleton will be left unpainted on the exterior, the special metal allowed to oxidize to a natural patina of dark red-brown. There is something almost brutal in this assertion of technical virtuosity. For sheer articulated power the Civic Center stands by itself among American skyscrapers, a statement of physical laws on a grand scale.

Across the street from the plaza of the Center stands the Brunswick Building, constructed at the same time as its neighbor to the north. Another triumph of SOM engineering, the Brunswick was the largest building at the time of its construction with load-bearing, screen walls of concrete, as they are awkwardly designated. A wall of this kind is the most recent structural innovation in American building and was developed to maintain uniform column spacing and window size while preserving relative freedom of interior planning. It was first used for the entire area of external walls in two large apartment projects designed by I. M. Pei—the Kips Bay Plaza group in New York and the University Apartments in Chicago, both erected in 1959–61. The application of the form to building walls may be thought of as a combination of the traditional masonry-bearing wall and the articulated or cellular curtain of the Chicago School. The aesthetic virtue of the load-bearing screen is that it brings back to the wall the texture, depth, and mass that we miss in the monotonous and brittle curtain of glass and enameled steel. Again, the interior of the Brunswick is column-free, and the elevator bays are enclosed in solid concrete walls which provide resistance to wind loads. The wall loads of the building are carried to the columns of the base by a peripheral girder 24 feet 5½ inches deep, occupying the combined height of the second and third stories.

In the conventional form of column-and-beam framing, Skidmore, Owings and Merrill used another extreme bay span in the United Air Lines building in Elk Grove. The 66-foot bays were made possible by the use of prestressed girders, one of the major building inventions of the twentieth century. The long bays and the two-story height give the UAL buildings an exaggerated horizontality, nicely appropriate to their open, level prairie setting.

Outside the ruling mode of structural expression there are other rediscoveries of the earlier Chicago work. The most welcome is the revival of the projecting bay, or oriel, that chiefly marked the hotels and apartments of the Chicago School. Two good examples stand among the imaginative designs of Harry Weese. The first is the apartment at 227 East Walton Street, opened in 1955, exactly planned for both light and privacy on a narrow lot and narrower street. More prominent because of its open site is Stanley R. Pierce Hall, completed in 1960 as a dormitory for the University of

Chicago. The oriel windows of this building were designed primarily to break up the flat curtain of brick and glass into a multiplicity of light-reflecting planes. The same device is used on a larger scale but less successfully in the long elevation of the Michigan Terrace Apartments, opened in 1963 at Michigan and Grand avenues. Here the projections are set so close together that each one in effect blocks out those on either side of it.

The towers of Bertrand Goldberg's Marina City, erected in 1960–64, constitute another stunning exhibition of structural virtuosity, but their background follows a different historical cycle. The cylindrical cores that share the vertical loads with the peripheral columns and provide resistance to the lateral forces of the wind go back to the principle of core-and-cantilever construction, which was first proposed by Mies van der Rohe in 1919 for a Berlin skyscraper that was never built, nor has it been used for any of his Chicago buildings. The system was first embodied in the Research Tower of S. C. Johnson and Company at Racine, Wisconsin (1947–50), designed by the former Chicagoan, Frank Lloyd Wright. Thus, partly by historical coincidence, this form also seems appropriate to the Chicago tradition.

While Marina City was under construction the whole inner city erupted into a building boom that produced a rapid succession of daring and heroically scaled architectural works. For all their diversity and novelty of form, however, they represent contemporary variations on the organic principle that the architects and engineers of Chicago had long ago developed into a fundamental working concept. The first phase of the University of Illinois Circle Campus, designed by Skidmore, Owings and Merrill, was opened in 1965, with the next phase continuing in construction through 1968. The buildings express the new interest in the plasticity of massive concrete; but in this case, the endless plastic possibilities, so tempting to other architects, have been disciplined by the rectilinear geometry of concrete framing. By 1968 the Lake Point Tower of Heinrich and

Schipporeit was completed, a curtain-walled skyscraper whose curving surfaces represent the first embodiment of the idea proposed by Mies in his Berlin project of 1921. The three-lobed shape of Lake Point has a sculptural quality unmatched in the conventional flat-plane construction; yet the form was not a matter of caprice but grew out of planning and structural as well as aesthetic considerations. The year following the opening of Lake Point saw the largest of all Chicago skyscrapers reach completion, to inaugurate another upward jump in the city's ever-expanding scale. The 850-foot First National Bank Building, with its outer columns sweeping upward in parabolic curves, was the joint product of the C. F. Murphy and the Perkins and Will offices. Rising to over 1,000 feet in height is the Hancock Center, another SOM masterpiece, in which a powerful sense of aerial movement is secured through the tapering form and the external diagonal bracing that leads the eye upward past story after story to the top.

To elucidate the full meaning of the new Chicago work for the general development of modern architecture would require an extensive historical and aesthetic analysis. It is possible, however, to get at the essence of it in a few generalizations. The great historical styles of architecture, as these appear in monumental works such as ecclesiastical and civic buildings, may be regarded in essence as the symbolic images of some kind of cosmos—divine, natural, or political, depending on the views of the age. In the absence of any public agreement on the nature of an encompassing order, modern architecture has repeated the history of the Chicago School in continuing its two basic approaches to formal design. One seeks a personal statement that increasingly moves toward plastic self-expression. This stream was long dominated by Frank Lloyd Wright, while after his death it came to be associated mainly with the pictorial formalism of architects such as Louis I. Kahn and Paul Rudolph. The other approach tries to find a more public and objective image, and by necessity turns to the laws of physical science as they are embodied in scientific structural design.

The second category is easily the larger of the two. Its pervasiveness is clearly attested by the influence of engineers like Pier Luigi Nervi and by the steady outpouring of books composed around the theme that structure and form are identical. But this form arises from the exigencies of utilitarianism and technical requirements and is thus essentially empirical. The new Chicago movement belongs in good part to the technological approach. Technical details are developed as symbols for the mathematical-scientific concepts underlying the structure. The emotional impact of such building arises mainly from the evocation of kinesthetic images; the experience it offers is a formal intensification of that provided by great engineering works such as bridges, dams, and other pure structural revelations.

Key to Buildings

The following is a list of the buildings illustrated in this guide. For easy reference, they have been grouped in five categories, as follows:

  I. Buildings of Architectural Merit in Historic Styles
 II. Buildings of the Chicago School
III. Buildings of the Prairie School
IV. Buildings of General Interest
 V. Recent Buildings

Buildings in the list and in the text are keyed to the general map of Chicago and suburbs (1) and to their respective area maps (2–6). Locations of the five area maps are shown on map 1. Works that have been officially selected as masterpieces of the Chicago School are designated by the letter L.

● **I. Buildings of Architectural Merit in Historic Styles**

	building	architect
1	St. Patrick's Church • 1854 718 W. Adams • Map 1	Unknown
2	Water Tower • 1869 N. Michigan at Chicago Map 2	W. W. Boyington
3	Giles Building • 1875 (now 423–29 S. Wabash Building) 423–29 S. Wabash • Map 3	Otis L. Wheelock
4	Florence Hotel (and Square) 1881 11111 S. Forrestville • Map 1	S. S. Beman

building	architect

5 Central Cold Storage
Warehouse • 1883
(originally the Hiram Sibley
Warehouse)
315–31 N. Clark • Map 3   George H. Edbrooke

6 Nickerson Residence • 1883
40 E. Erie • Map 2   Burling and Whitehouse

7 Grand Central Station • 1890
(originally Wisconsin Central
Station)
S. Wells at Harrison • Map 3   S. S. Beman

8 Fortnightly Club • 1892
(originally the Lathrop House)
120 E. Bellevue • Map 2   McKim, Mead and White

9 Holy Trinity Russian Orthodox
Cathedral • 1903
1121 N. Leavitt • Map 1   Louis H. Sullivan

10 Fourth Presbyterian Church and
Parish House • 1912
126 E. Chestnut • Map 2   R. A. Cram and H. V. Shaw

11 Rockefeller Memorial Chapel
1928
59th at Woodlawn • Map 5   Bertram W. Goodhue

◆ **II. Buildings of the Chicago School**

12 Leiter Building I • 1879 L
(now 208 West Monroe Building)
208 W. Monroe • Map 3   William L. Jenney

13 Glessner House • 1886 L
(now headquarters Chicago
School of Architecture
Foundation)
1800 S. Prairie • Map 4   Henry H. Richardson

14 Rookery Building • 1886 L
209 S. LaSalle • Map 3   Burnham and Root

building	architect
15 St. Gabriel's Church • 1887 4501 S. Lowe • Map 4	Burnham and Root
16 Wirt Dexter Building • 1887 L (now 630 South Wabash Building) 630 S. Wabash • Map 3	Adler and Sullivan
17 200 W. Adams Building • 1888 Map 3	Burling and Whitehouse
18 Auditorium Building • 1889 L (now Roosevelt University) S. Michigan at Congress Map 3	Adler and Sullivan
19 Getty Tomb • 1890 L Graceland Cemetery • Map 1	Louis H. Sullivan
20 Manhattan Building • 1890 431 S. Dearborn • Map 3	William L. Jenney
21 Monadnock Building • 1891 L 53 W. Jackson • Map 3	Burnham and Root
22 Sears, Roebuck and Co. 1891 L (originally Leiter Building II) Van Buren at State • Map 3	Jenney and Mundie
23 Sullivan House • 1892 L 4575 S. Lake Park • Map 4	Adler and Sullivan
24 Charnley House • 1892 L 1365 N. Astor • Map 2	Adler and Sullivan (Design: Frank Lloyd Wright)
25 Brewster Apartments • 1893 Diversey and Pine Grove Map 1	R. H. Turnock
26 Congress Hotel • 1893, 1902, 1907 504 S. Michigan • Map 3	Clinton J. Warren; Holabird and Roche
27 The Old Chicago Stock Exchange • 1894 L (now 30 North LaSalle Building) 30 N. LaSalle • Map 3	Adler and Sullivan

building	architect
28 Francis Apartments • 1895 L 4304 S. Forrestville • Map 4	Frank Lloyd Wright
29 Francisco Terrace Apartments 1895 253–57 N. Francisco • Map 1	Frank Lloyd Wright
30 Marquette Building • 1895 140 S. Dearborn • Map 3	Holabird and Roche
31 Reliance Building • 1895 L (now 32 North State Building) 32 N. State • Map 3	D. H. Burnham and Co.
32 Fisher Building • 1896 L 343 S. Dearborn • Map 3	D. H. Burnham and Co.
33 Heller House • 1897 L 5132 S. Woodlawn • Map 5	Frank Lloyd Wright
34 731 S. Plymouth Building 1897 (originally the Lakeside Press) Map 3	Howard V. Shaw
35 Gage Building • 1898 L 18 S. Michigan • Map 3	Holabird and Roche (Facade: Louis H. Sullivan)
36 Carson Pirie Scott Store 1899, 1903–4 L (originally the Schlesinger and Mayer Store) State at Madison • Map 3	Louis H. Sullivan
37 Crown Building • 1900 L (originally the McClurg Building) 218 S. Wabash • Map 3	Holabird and Roche
38 Schoenhofen Brewery Co. 1902 L (now Morningstar-Paisley Co.) 18th at Canalport • Map 4	Richard E. Schmidt (Design: Hugh Garden)
39 Madlener House • 1902 L (now the Graham Foundation) 4 W. Burton • Map 2	Richard E. Schmidt

	building	architect
40	Chapin and Gore Building 1904 L (now the 63 East Adams Building) 63 E. Adams • Map 3	Richard E. Schmidt
41	E-Z Polish Building • 1905 L (now Universal Foods Corp.) 3005 W. Carroll • Map 1	Frank Lloyd Wright
42	Magerstadt House • 1906 L 4930 S. Greenwood • Map 5	George W. Maher
43	Montgomery Ward and Co. Warehouse • 1907 618 W. Chicago • Map 1	Schmidt, Garden and Martin
44	Our Lady of Lebanon Church 1908 L (originally the First Congregational Church of Austin) Waller and Midway Park Map 1	Guenzel and Drummond
45	Liberty Mutual Insurance Building • 1908 L (originally the Hunter Building) 337 W. Madison • Map 3	Christian A. Eckstrom
46	Carl Schurz High School 1909 L Milwaukee at Addison • Map 1	Dwight H. Perkins
47	Robie House • 1909 L 5757 S. Woodlawn • Map 5	Frank Lloyd Wright
48	Grover Cleveland Elementary School • 1910 L 3850 N. Albany • Map 1	Dwight H. Perkins
49	Dwight Building • 1911 L 626 S. Clark • Map 3	Schmidt, Garden and Martin
50	City of Chicago Central Office Building • 1913 L (originally Reid, Murdoch and Co.) 325 N. LaSalle • Map 3	George C. Nimmons

building	architect
51 Park Buildings, Fuller Park 1915 45th and S. Princeton • Map 4	Edward H. Bennett
52 Krause Music Store • 1922 L (now Arnzen-Coleman Co.) 4611 N. Lincoln • Map 1	Louis H. Sullivan; William C. Presto
53 Third Unitarian Church • 1937 301 N. Mayfield • Map 1	Paul Schweikher, Inc.
54 University Building • 1937 L 5551 S. University • Map 5	G. Fred Keck and William Keck
55 Illinois Institute of Technology Campus • 1942–58 L 32d at State • Map 4	Mies van der Rohe; Friedman, Alschuler and Sincere; Holabird and Root; Pace Associates
56 Promontory Apartments • 1949 5530 South Shore • Map 5	Mies van der Rohe; Pace Associates; Holsman, Holsman and Klekamp
57 860–80 Lake Shore Drive Apartments • 1952 L Map 2	Mies van der Rohe; Pace Associates; Holsman, Holsman, Klekamp and Taylor
58 Inland Steel Building 1957 L 30 W. Monroe • Map 3	Skidmore, Owings and Merrill
59 Lake Meadows • 1956–60 31st to 35th and King Drive Map 4	Skidmore, Owings and Merrill

■ III. Buildings of the Prairie School

60 Wright House and Studio 1889–95 951 Chicago, Oak Park • Map 6	Frank Lloyd Wright
61 Winslow House • 1893 515 Auvergne, River Forest Map 6	Frank Lloyd Wright

building	architect
62 Willits House • 1902 1145 Sheridan, Highland Park Map 1	Frank Lloyd Wright
63 Brown House • 1905 2420 Harrison, Evanston Map 1	Frank Lloyd Wright
64 Glasner House • 1905 850 Sheridan, Glencoe • Map 1	Frank Lloyd Wright
65 Unitarian Universalist Church and Parish House (Unity Temple) • 1906 Lake at Kenilworth, Oak Park Map 6	Frank Lloyd Wright
66 Coonley House • 1908 300 Scottswood, Riverside Map 6	Frank Lloyd Wright
67 Drummond House • 1909 559 Edgewood, River Forest Map 6	William Drummond
68 Mrs. Thomas H. Gale House 1909 6 Elizabeth, Oak Park • Map 6	Frank Lloyd Wright
69 Carter House • 1910 1024 Judson, Evanston • Map 1	Walter Burley Griffin
70 Lewis House • 1940 Little St. Mary's Road, Libertyville • Map 1	Frank Lloyd Wright

▲ **IV. Buildings of General Interest**

71 Henry B. Clarke House • 1836 4526 S. Wabash • Map 4	Unknown
72 Holy Family Church • 1860 St. Ignatius High School (College) • 1869 1076 and 1072 W. Roosevelt Map 1	John M. Van Osdel (?) Unknown

	building	architect
73	First Congregational Church 1871 (originally the Union Park Congregational Church) 44 N. Ashland • Map 1	Gurdon P. Randall
74	Fine Arts Building • 1884 (originally the Studebaker Building) 410 S. Michigan • Map 3	S. S. Beman
75	The Art Institute • 1892 Michigan at Adams • Map 3	Shepley, Rutan and Coolidge
76	Newberry Library • 1892 60 W. Walton • Map 2	Henry I. Cobb
77	The Coliseum • 1900 1513 S. Wabash • Map 4	Frost and Granger
78	Wrigley Building • 1921, 1924 N. Michigan at the River Map 3	Graham, Anderson, Probst and White
79	Tribune Tower • 1925 N. Michigan at the River Map 3	Hood and Howells
80	Riverside Plaza • 1929 400 W. Madison • Map 3	Holabird and Root
81	John G. Shedd Aquarium 1929 S. Lake Shore at E. Roosevelt Map 4	Graham, Anderson, Probst and White
82	Merchandise Mart • 1929–30 North Bank of the River Map 3	Graham, Anderson, Probst and White
83	Playboy Building • 1929–30 919 N. Michigan • Map 2	Holabird and Root
84	Max Adler Planetarium • 1930 East end Achsah Bond • Map 4	Ernest Grunsfeld
85	Crow Island School • 1940 1112 Willow, Winnetka • Map 1	Eliel and Eero Saarinen; Perkins, Wheeler and Will

	building	architect
86	Sun-Times Building • 1957 N. Wabash at the River • Map 3	Naess and Murphy
87	Hyde Park Redevelopment 1959 55th and S. Lake Park • Map 5	I. M. Pei; Harry Weese; Loewenberg and Loewenberg
88	Chicago O'Hare International Airport • 1963 Northwest City Limits • Map 1	Naess and Murphy
89	Marina City • 1964,1967 River between State and Dearborn • Map 3	Bertrand Goldberg Associates
90	Federal Center • 1964 Dearborn from Adams to Jackson • Map 3	Mies van der Rohe; Schmidt, Garden and Erikson; C. F. Murphy Associates; A. Epstein and Sons
91	Civic Center • 1965 Randolph, Washington, Dearborn, and Clark • Map 3	C. F. Murphy Associates; Loebl, Schlossman and Bennett; Skidmore, Owings and Merrill
92	Equitable Building • 1965 N. Michigan at the River Map 3	Skidmore, Owings and Merrill; Alfred Shaw, Associated
93	University of Illinois Chicago Campus • 1965 Harrison and Halsted • Map 1	Skidmore, Owings and Merrill; C. F. Murphy Associates; A. Epstein and Sons
94	City Parking Facility ("Bird Cage") • 1954 11 W. Wacker • Map 3	Shaw, Metz and Dolio
95	Chess Pavilion, Lincoln Park 1956 Lincoln Park • Map 2	Morris Webster
96	Law School, University of Chicago • 1960 1121 East·60th • Map 5	Eero Saarinen
97	Atrium Houses • 1961 1370 E. Madison Park • Map 5	Y. C. Wong

★ **V. Recent Buildings**

building	architect
98 Hartford Insurance Building 1961 100 S. Wacker • Map 3	Skidmore, Owings and Merrill
99 Continental Insurance Building 1962 55 E. Jackson • Map 3	C. F. Murphy Associates
100 235 West Eugenie Street Apartments • 1962 Map 2	Harry Weese and Associates
101 United States Gypsum Building 1963 101 S. Wacker • Map 3	The Perkins and Will Partnership
102 Temple of North Shore Congregation Israel • 1963 1185 Sheridan, Glencoe • Map 1	Minoru Yamasaki
103 Loop Synagogue • 1963 16 S. Clark • Map 3	Loebl, Schlossman and Bennett
104 Emmanuel Presbyterian Church 1965 1850 S. Racine • Map 1	Loebl, Schlossman, Bennett and Dart
105 Sandburg Village • 1965, 1969 Clark, Division, La Salle, North • Map 2	Louis R. Solomon and John D. Cordwell
106 Raymond M. Hilliard Center 1966 Cermak at State • Map 4	Bertrand Goldberg Associates
107 Lutheran School of Theology 1967 55th at Greenwood • Map 5	The Perkins and Will Partnership
108 South Commons • 1967 Michigan, 26th, Prairie, 31st Map 4	Ezra Gordon and Jack M. Levin and Associates; L. R. Solomon–J. D. Cordwell Associates

	building	architect
109	Lake Point Tower • 1968 E. Grand and N. Lake Shore Map 1	Schipporeit–Heinrich Associates; Graham, Anderson, Probst and White
110	First National Bank Building 1969 Madison between Dearborn and Clark • Map 3	C. F. Murphy Associates; The Perkins and Will Partnership
111	John Hancock Center • 1969 Michigan between Chestnut and Delaware • Map 2	Skidmore, Owings and Merrill
112	McCormick Place • 1970 S. Lake Shore at 23d • Map 4	C. F. Murphy Associates

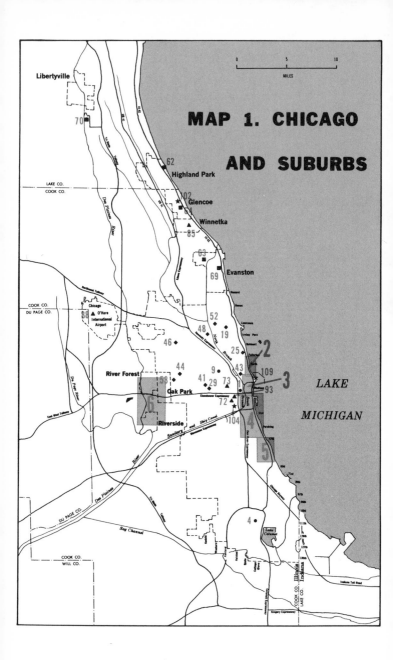

MAP 2.

NEAR NORTH

LAKE

MICHIGAN

LINCOLN PARK

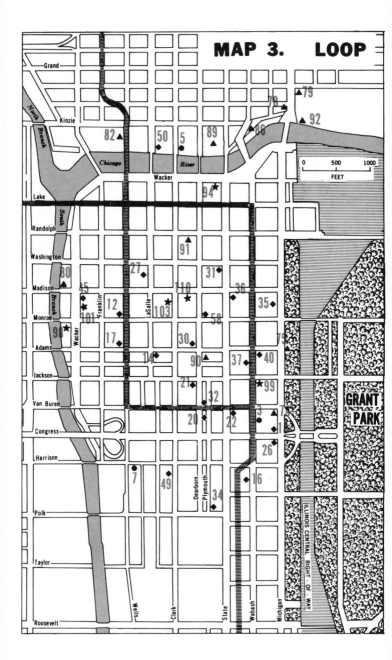

Roosevelt

Canal

Chicago River

Branch River

18th

38

Archer

13

106

Cermak

26th

31st

Dan Ryan Expwy

108

55

35th

ROCK ISLAND RIGHT · OF · WAY

Pershing

43d

28

MAP 4.
SOUTH SIDE

15

51

71

23

State

Indiana

King

47th

81

Planetarium

84

77

Meigs
Field
Airport

112

LAKE

MICHIGAN

59

Lake Shore Drive

Lake Park

0   1000   2000
FEET

ILLINOIS CENTRAL RIGHT · OF · WAY

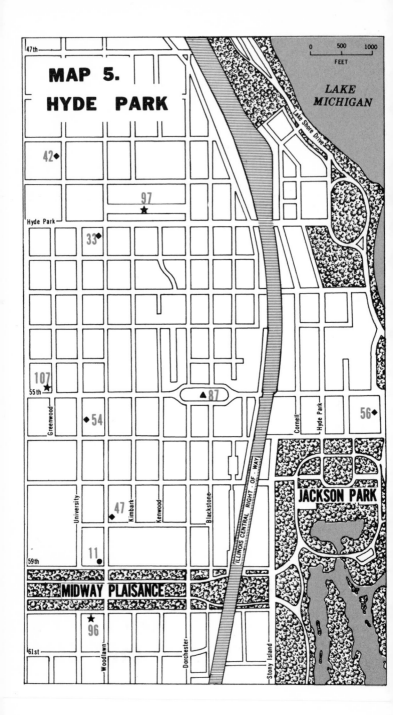

MAP 5.
HYDE PARK

LAKE
MICHIGAN

0   500   1000
FEET

47th

42◆

97
★

Hyde Park

33◆

Lake Shore Drive

107
★
55th

▲87

Greenwood

◆54

Cornell

Hyde Park

56◆

JACKSON PARK

University

47
◆

Kimbark

Kenwood

Blackstone

ILLINOIS CENTRAL RIGHT - OF - WAY

11
●
59th

MIDWAY PLAISANCE

96
★

Woodlawn

Dorchester

Stony Island

61st

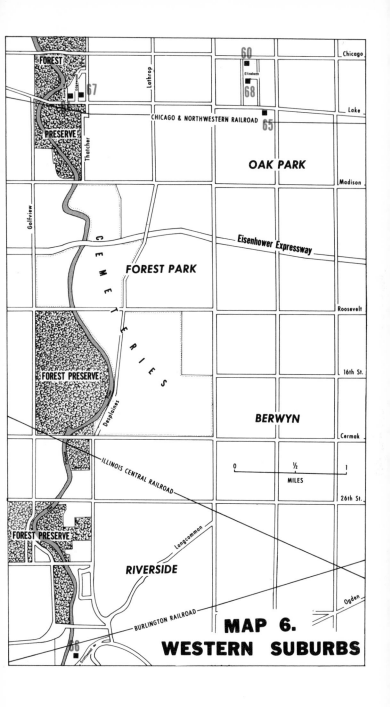

MAP 6.
WESTERN SUBURBS

1 St. Patrick's Church.   1854.   ●

Architect unknown.
718 West Adams (200 S). Map 1.

An early church in the Romanesque style (often
called Norman in the 1850's), exemplified by
round arches, narrow windows, and broad,
massive walls. Typical of this style also are the
arched "corbel-tables" (thickened horizontal
strips of wall, carried on masonry projections
called "corbels," here connected by small
arches against the wall). The small octagonal
towers are not ineffective, given the small scale
of all the elements—for instance, the narrow
arched windows (compare No. 71). Originally
the center of the facade ended in a gable at the
top, and there were no belfry stories or spires
on the towers (although they doubtless were
intended from the beginning).

2 **Water Tower. 1869.** ●

Architect: W. W. Boyington.
North Michigan (100 E) at Chicago (800 N).
Map 2.

An imitation of Gothic architecture so naïve that
it seems original at points, as in the cut-stone
"battlements" at the top of the lower wall
sections. Oscar Wilde, on his visit to Chicago in
1882, called it "a castellated monstrosity with
pepper boxes stuck all over it," although he
praised the pumping machinery as "simple,
grand and natural." Today it has the character
of a museum piece and is kept by Chicago on
its most prominent avenue in conscious
commemoration of the past. It is one of the rare
buildings, in the area burned over, to survive
the Great Fire of 1871.

3 Giles Building. 1875. ●

(Now the 423–29 South Wabash Building.)
Architect: Otis L. Wheelock.
423–29 South Wabash (45 E). Map 3.

Built just after the Fire, this is the most nearly
intact of the office buildings that followed French
fashion and were said to be in the "Mansard"
style. The top story of the Giles still has its
steeply pitched "roof-wall," or mansard. The
decorative motifs of a conventionalized running
vine *(rinceau)* and incised squares doubtless
were intended to remind art-lovers of the
elegance of buildings of the Second Empire in
France. (Demolished, 1968.)

4 Florence Hotel (and Square). 1881. ●

Architect: S. S. Beman.
11111 South Forrestville (523 E). Map 1.

The hotel is a fascinating relic of the times, as vivid as some newly made set for a story of the eighties. The square and the houses near it preserve much of the atmosphere of the original town. Built by the Pullman Company for its employees and laid out by Beman, Pullman is historically important as an example of the contemporary ideas on village or city planning.

5 Central Cold Storage Warehouse. 1883. ●

(Originally the Hiram Sibley Warehouse.)
Architect: George H. Edbrooke.
315–31 North Clark (100 W). Map 3.

The design suggests the structural bay, i.e., the
intervals between the supports. However, there
are naïve touches of ornament, and even more
naïve setting of piers or wall sections above
mullions (the more slender vertical dividers).
The river side was supported on thirty-foot oak
piles, the first known use of deep piles under
the wall of a building. Perhaps their use here
was inspired by previous use of such piles
under grain elevators along the river.

6 Nickerson Residence. 1883. ●

Architects: Burling and Whitehouse.
40 East Erie (658 N). Map 2.

One of the rich houses of the eighties and well
preserved, this classical structure, perhaps
inspired by Parisian townhouses, contrasts with
Burling's more direct treatment of a business
building, as seen in the 200 West Adams
Building (No. 17). The interiors offer fascinating
examples of the use of period styles in such
houses at the time. The owner was one of the
early art collectors of Chicago, and the Art
Institute of Chicago now has in its collections
works that doubtless appeared at one time in
the "gallery" that formed a part of this house.

7 **Grand Central Station.   1890.   ●**

(Originally Wisconsin Central Station.)
Architect: S. S. Beman.
South Wells (200 W) and Harrison (600 S).
Map 3.

The building is designed in a routine version of
the Romanesque style. Architecturally it is
noteworthy for the very fine tower. Structurally
it is noted as the first building to be built entirely
on long piles driven to a layer of stiff clay more
than fifty feet below the surface. Despite the
weight of the tower, this method prevented the
uneven settling which was a serious problem
for heavy buildings on the soft soil of Chicago
(see No. 18). The train shed is interesting as an
example of the glass and iron construction of
the time, allowing maximum lightness and
openness.

8 Fortnightly Club. 1892. ●

(Originally the Lathrop House.)
Architects: McKim, Mead and White.
120 East Bellevue (1031 N). Map 2.

An unusually fine facade in the classic manner,
related to the Georgian style of the eighteenth
century. The shallow relieving arches over the
openings of the first floor, the scale of the
decoration over the three central ones, the
relative emphasis in the two string courses and
the cornice, and the vigor given by the
projection of the ample bays at each end are
the most obvious features of a masterly design,
clear, open, urbane. In part because of the
placing of the door, the facade carries its
symmetry easily, without rigidity or undue
emphasis. The length of the central window of
the third floor, which breaks the string course
below the other windows here, was related to
a light, openwork balcony outside it, now
removed; similar balconies were outside the
three central windows of the second floor.

9 Holy Trinity Russian Orthodox Cathedral. 1903. ●

Architect: Louis H. Sullivan.
1121 North Leavitt (2200 W). Map 1.

Interesting as a work in a traditional form by
the "prophet of modern architecture." The basic
form is that of Russian churches, derived from
the earlier Byzantine architecture. The plan is a
central type, basically a square with extensions
at ground level, the central space crowned with
a dome. In the interior the proportions of the
space—small, but with relatively large arches—
the painted decoration, and the shallow dome
combine to produce an effect of delicacy and
refinement, as of a richly decorated coffer or
jewel box. The exterior is simple, with
occasional exotic touches in curved shapes or
angular window hoods. The exotic becomes
more obvious in the onion-like shape above the
lantern, which must be inspired by the bulbous
domes found in Russian church architecture.
Ornament is very sparingly used, the most
striking appearance being in the cut-out
ornament in wood over the entrance, similar to
that originally in the interior of the Carson Pirie
Scott Store (No. 36).

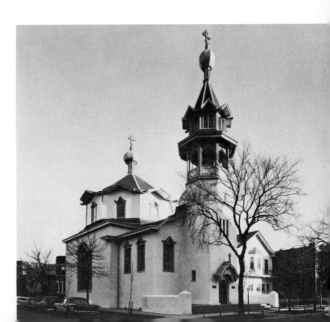

10 Fourth Presbyterian Church and Parish House. 1912. ●

Architects: Ralph A. Cram; Howard V. Shaw.
126 East Chestnut (860 N). Map 2.

The church is by one of the leaders of the Gothic revival in the United States, Ralph A. Cram, and the accurate knowledge of the Gothic style found in this building contrasts with the more naïve imitation in such earlier buildings as Holy Family (No. 72) or the Water Tower (No. 2). However, the Gothic features are often modified, as in the narrowness of the side aisles, the shape of the piers, and the use of the transept space for a balcony, suggesting that the architect allowed himself some degree of freedom. The severity of the exterior contrasts with the warmer and more varied wall surfaces in the adjacent Parish House by Howard V. Shaw.

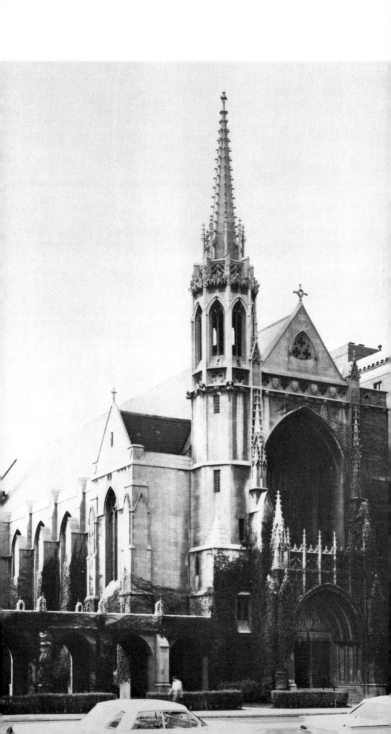

11 Rockefeller Memorial Chapel.   1928.   ●

Architect: Bertram W. Goodhue.
59th at Woodlawn (1200 E). Map 5.

An impressive example of the later Gothic
revival by one of its leading practitioners in the
United States. Its massive and solid character
contrasts with the lighter quality of the Fourth
Presbyterian Church (No. 10) by Goodhue's
former partner, Ralph A. Cram.

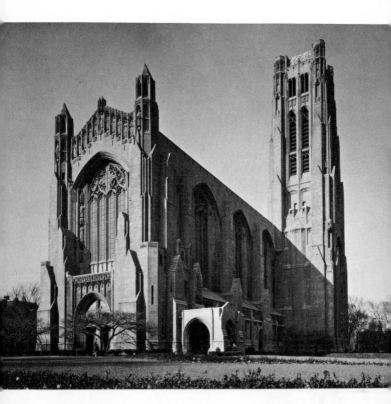

(Later the Morris Building, now the 208 West
Monroe Building.)
Architect: William L. Jenney.
208 West Monroe (100 S). Map 3.

The citation by the Landmarks Commission
reads: "In recognition of its contribution towards
the development of skeleton construction. Cast
iron pilasters continue as columns from
foundation to roof, with widely spaced piers
framing glass bays, which anticipate the steel
cage of the Chicago School." The floor beams
are carried by cast-iron columns set against the
brick piers of the facade, and thus the piers,
relieved of part of their usual load, could be
made narrower than would otherwise have been
possible. The mullions (the narrower vertical
members separating the individual windows) are
also of cast iron. The aim of the architect in all
this was not so much to develop any new style
or conception of architectural effect, but simply
to get more light into the offices.

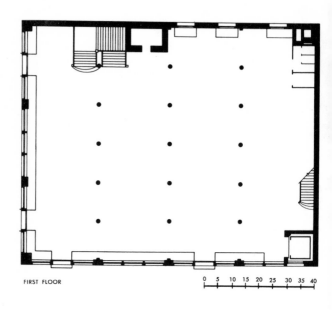

FIRST FLOOR

0 5 10 15 20 25 30 35 40

FIFTH FLOOR

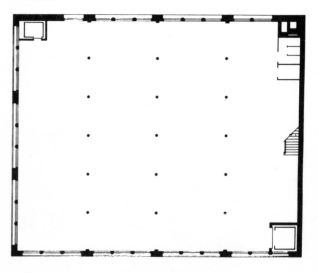

64

Leiter Building I

13 Glessner House. 1886. ◆   **L**

(Now headquarters of the Chicago
School of Architecture Foundation.)
Architect: H. H. Richardson.
1800 South Prairie (300 E). Map 4.

The citation by the Landmarks Commission
effectively sums up the achievement in this
wonderfully sturdy and solid house: "In
recognition of the fine planning for an urban
site, which opens the family rooms to the quiet
serenity of an inner yard; the effective ornament
and decoration; and the impressive
Romanesque masonry, expressing dignity and
power." The north wall, with its powerful arch,
is a fine example of Richardson's handling of
masonry. The Glessner House is of especial
interest as the only surviving example in
Chicago of the work of one of the greatest
American architects.

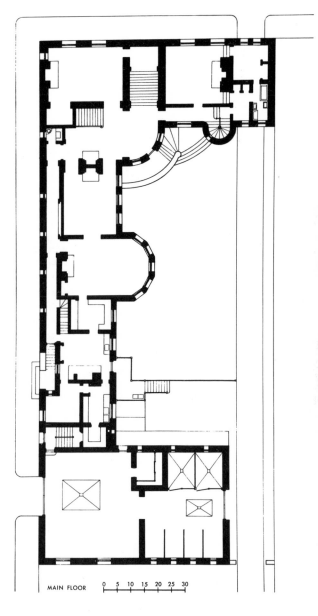

MAIN FLOOR   0 5 10 15 20 25 30

Glessner House

69

14 Rookery Building. 1886. ◆ L

Architects: Burnham and Root.
209 South LaSalle (150 W). Map 3.

The citation by the Landmarks Commission
reads: "In recognition of its pioneering plan in
providing shops and offices around a graceful
semi-private square and the further development
of the skeleton structural frame using cast iron
columns, wrought iron spandrel beams, and
steel beams to support party walls and interior
floors." (The ground story of the "court" was
remodeled by Frank Lloyd Wright in 1905.) A
noteworthy combination of strength and grace
is achieved in the design. The ornament is very
interesting, especially its placement: in most
cases it emphasizes architectural features, such
as the floor lines within the larger openings, or
the place where a capital might be; but in other
cases it seems to be addressed simply, and
courteously, to the spectator's enjoyment. The
vigorous contrast of columns and heavy
stonework is more effective and more unified
than in the Fine Arts Building (No. 74). This
contrast, the massive walls combined with large
windows, the degree of emphasis at the corners,
top, and center of the facade, all help to
establish this building's strong presence. Root
held that the virtues of architecture were similar
to the traits of civilized people, and the Rookery
can well be viewed in this way. It stands there
like a stronghearted and cheerful person,
forceful yet friendly.

Rookery Building

73

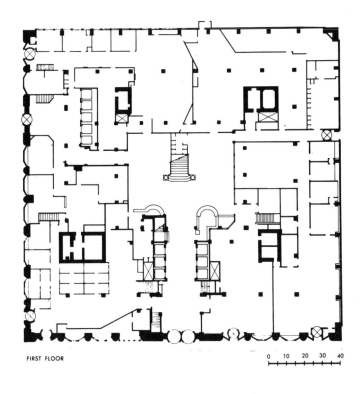

FIRST FLOOR

0 10 20 30 40

Rookery Building

15 St. Gabriel's Church. 1887. ◆

Architects: Burnham and Root.
4501 South Lowe (632 W). Map 4.

This building is remarkable in the bold, broad massing of the chief elements, including the chapels at the back. The effect of breadth and strength is emphasized by the subtle batter (the inward slope of the wall as it rises), nicely worked out in the brick at the foot of the walls. The tower has been lowered by the removal of a section that was just below the present top story, and the latter has been rebuilt in line with the lower stories, whereas it originally projected beyond them. The tower has thus lost in force as well as in height. The present entrance porch has been added, and there are minor changes, as in the buttresses. The interior maintains its original breadth and spaciousness, owing to the broad vaulted shapes of the ceiling, although there has been some remodeling, especially in the northern part. Despite changes, the building still has a degree of individuality and character recalling the Rookery (No. 14), by the same architects. (The date is on the cornerstone.)

16 Wirt Dexter Building. 1887. ◆   L

(Now the 630 South Wabash Building.)
Architects: Adler and Sullivan.
630 South Wabash (45 E). Map 3.

The narrow mullions, in the central bay, with
the slight moldings crossing them give a touch
of distinction to the otherwise very simple
treatment of a commercial building. (The central
section originally ended in a low gable at the
top of the facade.) At the back is an interesting
use of openwork iron members set outside the
"wall," presumably to conserve space inside.

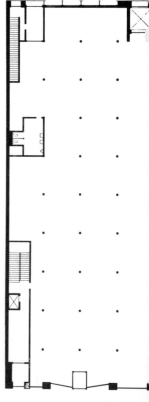

0 5 10 15 20 25

17 200 West Adams Building. 1888. ◆

Architects: Burling and Whitehouse.
200 West Adams (200 S). Map 3.

A sober, effective design for an office building,
this represents the better commercial
architecture of the time, comparing favorably,
for instance, with Sullivan's design for the Wirt
Dexter Building (No. 16). The slight rounding
of the corners of the piers subtly emphasizes
their mass.

18 Auditorium Building. 1889. ◆   **L**

(Now Roosevelt University.)
Architects: Adler and Sullivan.
S. Michigan 100 E) and Congress (500 S)
(NW corner). Map 3.

One of Chicago's most famous cultural and
architectural landmarks. The citation of the
Landmarks Commission reads: "In recognition
of the community spirit which here joined
commercial and artistic ends, uniting hotel,
office building, and theatre in one structure; the
inventiveness of the engineer displayed from
foundations to the perfect acoustics; and the
genius of the architect which gave form and,
with the aid of original ornament, expressed the

spirit of festivity in rooms of great splendor."
The exterior walls, which are traditional,
load-bearing walls, reveal a powerful rhythm of
limestone piers surmounting a rugged granite
base. In the interior, especially in the theater,
there is an intricate system of iron framing that,
among other things, carried the kitchen and the
banquet hall on trusses above the stage and
the auditorium. In the interior is much of
Sullivan's elaborate ornament to delight the eye.

A hidden drama was played out over a period
of many years in the foundations. Heavy
buildings were expected to settle a good deal,
given the soft soil of Chicago; and the
foundations of the Auditorium consisted of
spread footings containing layers of railroad
rails and I-beams embedded in concrete,
proportioned to the expected loads, and
intended to equalize the settlement. The design
of the building, however, with its heavy walls
and much heavier tower, placed widely varying
loads on the foundations; and, despite the
ingenious plans of the engineers, the settlement
was very uneven. Distortion of the frame was
great, but the structure held, although
substantial settlement continued until around
1925. The experience demonstrated the need
for deep foundations under such heavy
buildings, either long piles (see No. 7) or
caissons (see No. 27). The theater has been
restored under the sponsorship of the
Auditorium Theater Council.

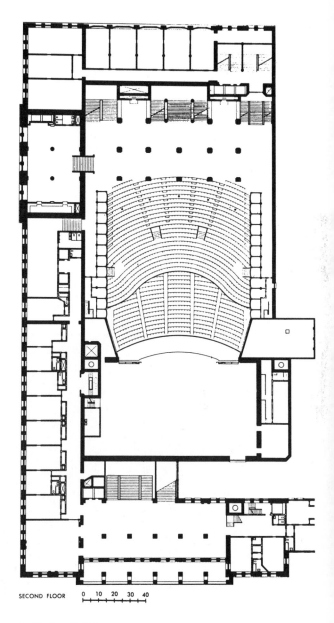

SECOND FLOOR   0 10 20 30 40

Auditorium Building

19 Getty Tomb. 1890. ◆   **L**

Graceland Cemetery.
Architect: Louis H. Sullivan.
4001 North Clark (100 W). Map 1.

The citation by the Landmarks Commission
reads: "In recognition of the design which here
brings new beauty to an age-old form: the tomb.
Stone and bronze stand transformed in rich yet
delicate ornament, a requiem for the dead, an
inspiration to the living." The ornament cut on
the stone is remarkable for the way in which an
apparently routine geometrical motif, a spokelike
figure inside an octagon, becomes, when
repeated, a decoration of the greatest delicacy,
like an openwork veil drawn over the solid
stone. Aside from the scale and the degree of
relief, which are fundamental, the execution of
the "spokes" in successive series of small balls
contributes a great deal to the delicacy and life
of this ornament. The bronze doors contain
some of Sullivan's finest ornament, with the
spokelike motif of the stone ornament above
subtly echoed within the rich floral design.

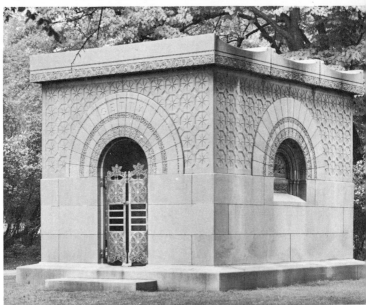

20 Manhattan Building. 1890. ◆

Architect: William L. Jenney.
431 South Dearborn (36 W). Map 3.

This and Burnham and Root's Rand McNally Building were the first tall office buildings to use skeleton construction throughout. Even the party walls are carried by the steel frame, in this case on beams cantilevered out, i.e., extending beyond their supporting columns. The building thus displays Jenney's interest in structural matters and his inventiveness in using the new material, iron or steel. The design, however, is not particularly impressive. The various materials and the different shapes in the bay windows, for instance, tend to produce an effect of indecision.

21 Monadnock Building. 1891. ◆   **L**

Architects: Burnham and Root.
53 West Jackson (300 S). Map 3.

The citation by the Landmarks Commission
reads: "In recognition of its original design and
its historical interest as the highest wall-bearing
structure in Chicago. Restrained use of brick,
soaring massive walls, omission of ornamental
forms, unite in a building simple yet majestic."
The extreme thickness of the walls (six feet at
ground level) showed that to go higher in
traditional masonry construction was not
feasible; the time had come for the introduction
of iron, and then steel, as the essential materials
for tall buildings. Noteworthy is the movement
given to the walls by the curvature inward above
the first story and out again at the top, with
the corners "chamfered" off.

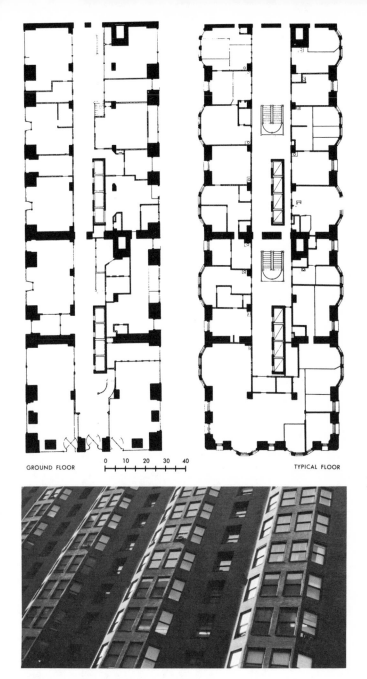

GROUND FLOOR

0 10 20 30 40

TYPICAL FLOOR

Monadnock Building

22   Sears, Roebuck and Company.   1891.   ◆

(Originally Leiter Building II.)
Architects: Jenney and Mundie.
State and Van Buren (400 S) (SE corner).
Map 3.

An example of the "commercial style" for which
Chicago was famous. The piers are narrow
enough to suggest the metal frame within them,
as do the slender piers and high ceilings of
the interior. Ornament is sparse, economy is
suggested, and the general effect is simple and
direct (more so than in the slightly later Fair
Building, by the same architects, on the NW
corner at State and Adams).

23 Sullivan House. 1892. ◆   L

Architects: Adler and Sullivan.
4575 South Lake Park (about 1200 E). Map 4.

A noteworthy example of a city house by Adler
and Sullivan. The blocky character of the stone
facade is similar to that of the Charnley House
(No. 24), and, since Wright apparently designed
the domestic structures for the firm, it is
possible that the design is his. The rich
ornament over the door suggests Sullivan. The
other ornamentation on the facade was removed
by vandals in 1964. Louis Sullivan lived in this
house during part of the nineties, the high point
of his architectural career. It is now occupied
by a volunteer welfare group, which has
undertaken to rehabilitate it.

24 Charnley House. 1892. ◆ **L**

Architects: Adler and Sullivan;
Frank Lloyd Wright.
1365 North Astor (50 E). Map 2.

Officially by the firm of Adler and Sullivan, this
house is believed to have been designed by
Wright while in their employ. The closed-up,
blocky design is in marked contrast to Wright's
later "prairie" houses (see No. 47). The shallow
brick and cut stone are the background for the
very formal design, of which the obvious
elements are the door and the small windows.
The balcony, in its lightness and openness,
contrasts with the solid mass of the house.
Despite its shallowness, one may ask whether
it perhaps puts an excessive emphasis on the
center of a short facade (contrast No. 8). A
later extension of the facade to the right, in the
porches built there, obscures its original
symmetry.

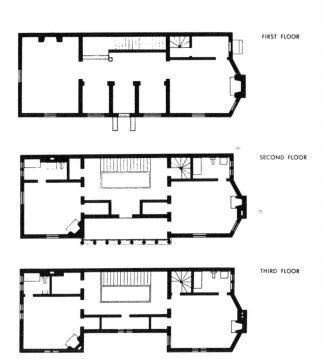

FIRST FLOOR

SECOND FLOOR

THIRD FLOOR

25 Brewster Apartments. 1893. ◆

Architect: R. H. Turnock.
Diversey (2800 N) and Pine Grove (600 W).
Map 1.

The narrow windows and the rough-faced
granite blocks of the wall make the Brewster
in its external appearance a rather traditional
and somewhat romanticized version of the
oriel-windowed apartment buildings of the
Chicago School. The interior design, however,
represents a bold solution to the problem of
admitting natural light to the spaces inside the
building. In plan it is a hollow rectangle, the
inner court of which is surmounted by a gabled
skylight—a common form for the multistory
office block in the late 19th century, but one
which posed a peculiar difficulty in the case of
an apartment building. To provide access to
upper-floor apartments from a single centrally
located elevator. Turnock introduced a little
pedestrian bridge running the length of the
court in each floor, with laterial branches
extending to the individual entrance doors. The
bridge decks are composed of glass blocks
supported by light, steel girders at the edges.
The thin frames of these translucent bridges
and the open grillwork of the elevator shaft
form a vivid pattern of black lines set off against
the diffused light falling from the glass roof
above the court.

26 Congress Hotel. 1893, 1902, 1907. ◆

Architects: Clinton J. Warren; Holabird and Roche.
504 South Michigan (100 E). Map 3.

The architects of the Chicago School created the modern hotel and apartment building as well as the office block, and the Congress is the best and largest of the multiple-dwelling structures. The vertical banks of projecting windows (called oriels), a distinguishing feature of many Chicago hotels and office buildings, allow the maximum admission of light, at the same time imparting to the long street elevations a vigorous sense of rhythmic movement. The broad openings of the base and the light screen-like walls clearly suggest a thin curtain drawn over the columns and girders of the steel frame. The original rough-faced granite blocks of the first story and the shape of the paired windows in the upper three stories indicate that Warren was deliberately trying to harmonize the initial block of the hotel with the Auditorium Building (No. 18) immediately to the north.

27 The Old Chicago Stock Exchange. 1894. ◆   **L**

(Now the 30 North LaSalle Building.)
Architects: Adler and Sullivan.
30 North LaSalle (150 W). Map 3.

The treatment of the wall above the third story
is noteworthy, the facets of the projecting bays
making an effective contrast with the plane of
the wall, which is emphasized by the larger
windows and their framing strips. The
proportions of the design have been criticized,
for instance, for the great height of the "base,"
which includes three stories. Doubtless Sullivan
wished to consider the trading room a part of
the "base," since this important room was
reached by a stairway directly from the street
level. It was on the second floor and was two
stories high. The tall arches which link the
second- and third-floor windows thus "express"
this high room (although it was in the center of
the building and not immediately behind these
windows). The running pattern of the ornament
just above the arches has a wonderful

movement in its curving forms, and its flat surface makes it admirably suited to a wall. Perhaps the entrance piece breaks uncomfortably into the second- and third-story band, but the arch itself is majestic. (The relief in the left-hand medallion represents the house of P. F. W. Peck, 1837, which originally stood on this site; the right-hand medallion contains the year in which the present building was begun, 1893.)

The first "caisson" foundations in Chicago were used under the west wall of this building. They were devised by General Sooy Smith, an engineer who was the chief authority on foundations in Chicago at this time. These caissons consisted of deep wells sunk here to hard clay, the sides of the wells being held in place by wood sheathing and steel rings until they were filled with concrete. They thus supported the building in the same manner as the long wood piles that had been used elsewhere (see No. 7), but they avoided the shock and vibration caused to immediately adjacent buildings by the driving of the long piles.

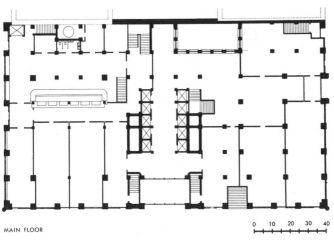

0 10 20 30 40

The Old Chicago Stock Exchange

Architect: Frank Lloyd Wright.
4304 South Forrestville (532 E). Map 4.

This apartment building is an interesting example of Wright's early work. In character it has the simple blockiness of the Charnley House (No. 24). The balconies on the facade offer a striking illustration of the effect of relationships on individual forms. If we look at only one of the wings, the balcony seems to be an excessive emphasis on the center of a short facade; but when the two wings are seen together, the balconies take their places as quite acceptable emphases on either side of the deep penetration of the "court" between the wings. The ornament follows Sullivan's geometrical (rather than his floral) type and creates very interesting variations on the theme of the circle.

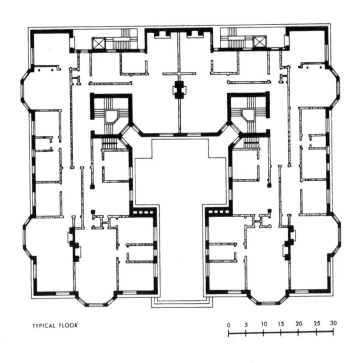

TYPICAL FLOOR

0 5 10 15 20 25 30

Francis Apartments

103

29 Francisco Terrace Apartments.   1895. ◆

Architect: Frank Lloyd Wright.
253–57 North Francisco (2900 W). Map 1.

Wright's answer to the problem of the
lower-priced apartment building at this time.
Although he omits the extensive ornament of
the Francis Apartments (No. 28), even here the
artist appears, as in the purely aesthetic
paneling of the brick on the west front, which,
however, does not detract from the
"monumental dignity and simplicity" of this
low-cost housing.

30 Marquette Building. 1895. ◆

Architects: Holabird and Roche.
140 South Dearborn (36 W). Map 3.

Despite the conventional cornice, the Marquette
is one of the least old-fashioned in appearance
and still one of the finest office buildings in
Chicago. Top and bottom follow Sullivan's idea
of setting off the first two and the topmost
stories from the others—with the addition here
of a transitional story, as it were, in each case.
The fine proportions of the windows, the
vigorous projection of the piers, and the
effective simple patterning of the piers of the
end bays combine to give the building its strong
yet pleasing character. The very end bay on
Adams Street is a later addition of 1905, and
outside the original design. The bronze reliefs
above the entrance, by American sculptor
Hermon A. MacNeil, portray incidents from the
life of Père Marquette.

Reliance Building. 1895. ◆   **L**

(Now the 32 North State Building.)
Architects: D. H. Burnham and Company.
32 North State. Map 3.

The citation by the Landmarks Commission
reads: "In recognition of the early and complete
expression, through slender piers, small
spandrels, and the skillfully restrained use of
terra cotta with large areas of glass, of the
structural cage of steel that alone supports
such buildings." The strength and convenience
of steel construction were shown in the
piecemeal manner in which this building was
put up. In 1890 John Root designed a

sixteen-story building for this site, but only the foundations and first story were built then. These were "slipped under" the upper stories of a four-story, heavy masonry building already there, the upper stories continuing in use during the process. In 1894 these older stories were "knocked off" and the present building carried on up. The designer in charge in 1894–95 was Charles Atwood, of D. H. Burnham and Company, who apparently redesigned the exteriors. It was at this time that the terra-cotta sheathing was designed. The moldings executed in the terra cotta accentuate the slenderness of the verticals and thus contribute to the sense of openness in the facades.

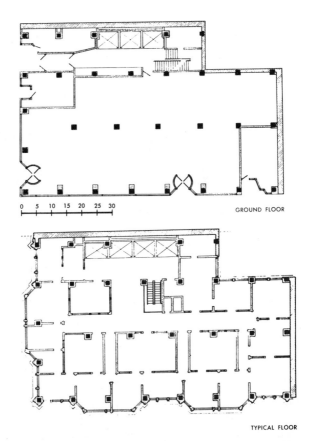

0 5 10 15 20 25 30

GROUND FLOOR

TYPICAL FLOOR

32 Fisher Building. 1896. ◆   L

Architects: D. H. Burnham and Company.
343 South Dearborn (36 W). Map 3.

An early example of the application of Gothic style to the skyscraper. The detail is consistently Gothic in inspiration, and the corner piers are even given the form of Gothic piers with engaged colonnettes (or moldings). One may note the emphasis on height which this accomplishes, aided here by the verticals of the projecting bays. The design achieves a notable openness and lightness, hardly inferior to the Reliance Building (No. 31), and thus vigorously expresses the steel frame despite the presence of the historical detail.

0 10 20 30 40

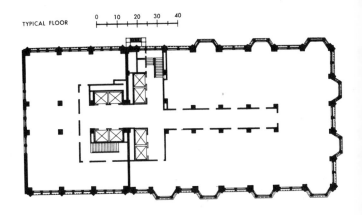

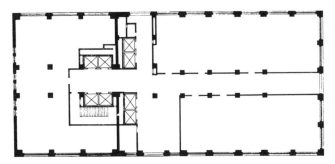

GROUND FLOOR

33 Heller House. 1897. ◆   **L**

Architect: Frank Lloyd Wright.
5132 South Woodlawn (1200 E). Map 5.

A notable example of Wright's work at this
time. Still quite blocklike and closed up below,
like many of his earlier houses, it is more open
on the upper floor and shows a more
interesting silhouette than the Charnley House
(No. 24). The lightening and opening of the
upper part foreshadows his later designs. The
molded plaster frieze at the top is by sculptor
Richard Bock.

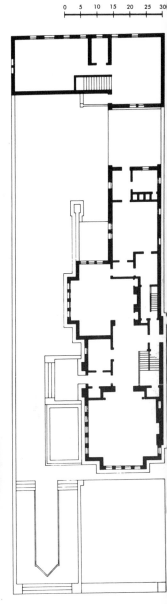

34 731 South Plymouth Building. 1897. ◆

(Originally the Lakeside Press Building.)
Architect: Howard V. Shaw.
731 South Plymouth (31 W). Map 3.

A vigorous design of generally traditional
character, but freely treated so that it seems
original rather than imitative. The facade gains
interest from the way the arches over some of
the openings are played off against the flat
heads, or lintels, of others and the greater
openness of the upper stories against the
greater solidness of the lower two. The
spandrels (horizontal strips of wall at the floor
levels) in the upper stories, and the window
glass throughout, are set well back from the
surfaces of the piers so as to show their mass,
which contributes greatly to the vigor and
strength of the whole design. The centerpiece,
around the doors, is interesting in its
modifications of classical motifs. The
coat-of-arms, with its Indian head and the
representation of Fort Dearborn in relief, and
the medallions refer to series of books
published by the Lakeside Press.

Gage Building. 1898. ◆ L

Architects: Holabird and Roche;
Louis H. Sullivan.
18 South Michigan (100 E). Map 3.

Only the facade was designed by Sullivan. The
citation by the Landmarks Commission refers
to it: ''In recognition of the fine relations
established between piers, windows, and wall
surfaces; the excellence of proportions
throughout; and the imaginative use of original
ornament.'' Sometimes Sullivan's ornament
seems plastered on at spots, rather than
integrated with a building, and the two bursts of
ornament at the tops of the piers suggest as
much, in this instance. Note, however, that the
architect designed an eight-story facade, the
other four stories being added later, in 1902.
Comparison of photographs taken before and
after suggests, surprisingly, that these
ornaments were perhaps ''held in'' better in the
smaller facade. There was also a band of rich,

though more delicate, ornament along the top
of the first story, which probably helped. The
two buildings to the south, 30 and 24 South
Michigan, were done entirely by Holabird and
Roche. Their facades form an interesting
contrast with the facade of the Gage Building.
The basic design is the same, but they do not
have the refinement and elegance of
proportion and accent to be found in the Gage.
In their avoidance of ornament they seem to
look to the future more directly than does
Sullivan's design.

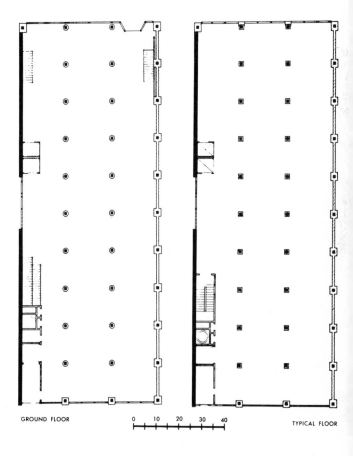

GROUND FLOOR   0   10   20   30   40   TYPICAL FLOOR

Gage Building

115

36 Carson Pirie Scott Store.
1899, 1903-4. ◆   L

(Originally the Schlesinger and Mayer Store.)
Architect: Louis H. Sullivan.
State and Madison (SE corner). Map 3.

The easternmost section of three bays on
Madison Street was built first, and the main
section, extending around the corner and with
seven bays on State Street, several years later.
(The third section was done by D. H. Burnham
and Company in 1906, and the southernmost by
Holabird and Root in 1960–61.) The wide
windows and narrow piers express the steel
frame, but the details suggest the sensitive
designer above all. The fine proportions of the
window openings, the firm emphasis in the
moldings around them, the accent given by the
line of delicate ornament on the horizontal wall
sections, all contribute to a perfection of design
rarely to be found. The rich ornament of the first
and second floors has been criticized as too
ornate for a commercial building. One should
note, however, that Sullivan held that the display

windows were like pictures and deserved rich
frames, and his prophetic power is seen in this,
if one compares old photographs showing
the stodgy displays of the time with
window-dressers' art of today. The citation by
the Landmarks Commission reads: ''In
recognition of the fine expression of interior
spaces in the serene horizontals of window and
wall; the execution of an original system of
ornament, and the excellent craftsmanship
of its execution in cast-iron.''

As in many of the older buildings, the original
projection, or cornice, at the top has been
replaced by a bald parapet. The large festoons
of ornament which were originally set outside
the piers between the first and second floors
have also been removed. (One wonders whether
they could ever have seemed very closely
related to the wall, rather than ''hung on'' it.)
They contained the initials ''SM'' for the owners.
The architect's initials ''LHS'' can still be seen
in some of the ornament, perhaps slipped in
by George G. Elmslie, who, as Sullivan's chief
designer, carried out much of the ornamental
design.

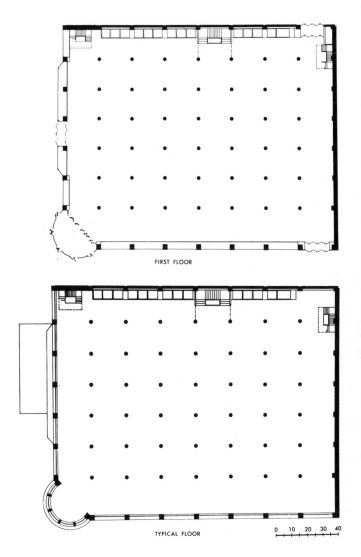

FIRST FLOOR

TYPICAL FLOOR

0 10 20 30 40

Carson Pirie Scott Store

37 Crown Building. 1900. ◆   L

(Originally the McClurg Building.)
Architects: Holabird and Roche.
218 South Wabash (45 E). Map 3.

Remarkable for the light and open character of
the facade. A fascinating study of design, for
instance, the relative emphasis on the horizontal
versus the vertical and on openness versus
solidness, is offered by comparison of the
treatment of the wall in this building with that
in the Marquette Building (No. 30) and the
Carson Pirie Scott Store (No. 36). The three
also offer interesting comparisons of the
treatment of the "Chicago windows," that is,
windows in which a fixed center light or lights
are flanked by movable sashes at the sides.

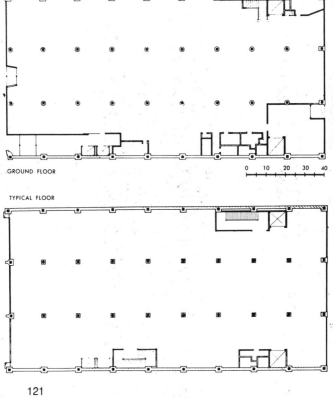

GROUND FLOOR

0 10 20 30 40

TYPICAL FLOOR

121

38 Schoenhofen Brewery Building.   1902.   ◆   L

(Now the Morningstar-Paisley Company.)
Architects: Richard E. Schmidt; Hugh Garden.
West 18th and Canalport (1800 S)
(NE corner). Map 4.

An interesting example on the work of the group
of architects who were developing a
non-historical approach at the beginning of the
century. In this building there is a fine
appreciation of the qualities of brick and
considerable inventiveness in attaining accents
or emphases by the way it is laid. Although
Schmidt was the commissioned architect, the
design was apparently made by Hugh Garden,
who was occasionally retained by Schmidt for
a given design for 1906, the year they formed
a partnership.

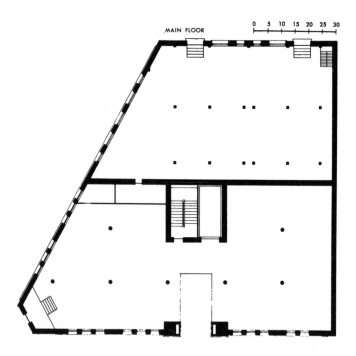

MAIN FLOOR   0   5   10   15   20   25   30

39 Madlener House. 1902. ◆   **L**

(Now the Graham Foundation for
Advanced Studies in the Fine Arts.)
Architect: Richard E. Schmidt.
4 West Burton (1500 N). Map 2.

A clear, cubical mass, as forceful as a
Florentine palace. There is an interesting variety
in the various emphases on the horizontal, in
stone base, string courses, and grouping of the
windows. The decoration around the door is a
fine piece of modern ornament, similar to
Sullivan's geometric type. The interior has been
remodeled and restored for the Graham
Foundation by Brenner, Danforth and Rockwell.

40 Chapin and Gore Building.   1904. ◆   L

(Later the Nepeenauk Building, now the
63 East Adams Building.)
Architect: Richard E. Schmidt.
63 East Adams (200 S). Map 3.

There is an originality almost mannerist here,
as in the split window-framing panels on the
second floor, contrasting with the beautifully
simple piers above; these piers then flowered
at the top into the "upside-down capitals," as
they were called when first seen. Unfortunately
they have been removed. Also the original
cornice has been replaced with a parapet, and
this, with the absence of the original capitals,
makes the upper part of the building
incongruously bare in relation to the lower part.

41 E-Z Polish Building. 1905. ◆   L

(Now the Universal Foods Corporation.)
Architect: Frank Lloyd Wright.
3005 West Carroll (338 N). Map 1.

Little remains of the original design here. The
building has been enlarged, the windows filled
up, and the original open stair-towers at the
ends closed. The interior has been remodeled
and the original surfaces covered.

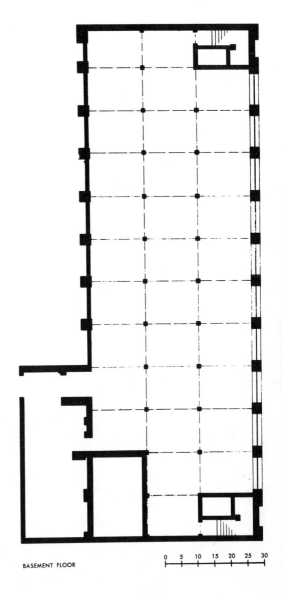

BASEMENT FLOOR

0 5 10 15 20 25 30

42 Magerstadt House. 1906. ◆ L

Architect: George W. Maher.
4930 South Greenwood (1100 E). Map 5.

A design by one of the architects who were
co-workers or assistants of Frank Lloyd Wright.
Very shallow brick, with subtle emphasis by
projection here and there, is used in a design
which consistently emphasizes a more massive
quality than is found in Wright's contemporary
houses. Perhaps, too, there is more obvious
recollection of other styles: the profile of the
cornice of the porch and the small rectangular
blocks or "dentils" under it remind one of
classical forms, and the foliate ornament on the
capitals of the columns perhaps recalls the Art
Nouveau decoration at the turn of the century.
The long plan and the entrance at the side of
the city lot will be found in Wright's Robie
House (No. 47); however, the frame around the
entrance is more massive and less integrated
with the rest of the building than in Wright's
famous work.

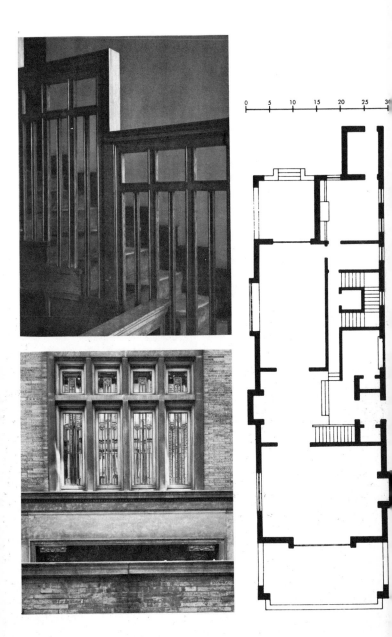

43 Montgomery Ward and Company Warehouse. 1907. ◆

Architects: Schmidt, Garden and Martin.
618 West Chicago (800 N). Map 1.

A warehouse which attains conscious and distinct architectural quality. An enormous and massive structure is given life by the movement in the spandrels (horizontal wall sections) accented by the projecting strips at top and bottom. (Brick facing on these sections accentuated their horizontal form in contrast to the piers, but they have lost this effect through being painted.) One should not overlook the ornament, a rosette-like form at the top of the verticals, and a swordlike motif at the top of the second story. The sober effect of strength is a good expression of the reinforced concrete construction. (The calculations for the loads carried in the structure were taken by Richard Schmidt from German technical publications with which he was familiar, since a reinforced concrete frame of this type had not been used before this by Chicago architects.)

44 Our Lady of Lebanon Church. 1908. ◆ L

(Originally the First Congregational
Church of Austin.)
Architects: Guenzel and Drummond.
Waller (5700 W) and Midway Park (500 N).
Map 1.

Standing in what was originally the suburb of
Austin, this church is a fine example of the work
of the Chicago School some of whose
members, as in this case, are almost forgotten.
Through the fine composition of rectangular
masses in brick, the "nave," or central part of
the interior, is well expressed, as are also the
lower "side-aisles." Without the ingenuity, or
the complicated character, of Wright's Unity
Temple in Oak Park, the interior is spacious
and serene, and can bear comparison very well.

Liberty Mutual Insurance   **L**
Building.   1908. ◆

(Originally the Hunter Building.)
Architect: Christian A. Eckstrom.
337 West Madison. Map 3.

This building represents the typical level of
achievement in the office building, as carried
on by many architects. Here there are direct
expression of the skeleton frame of steel and
the suggestion of plenty of light in the offices.
However, the way in which the building
continues above the cornice at the top of the
tenth story is disconcerting, as if the projected
height had been changed during the
construction. The variation in quality in these
generally satisfactory buildings is seen by
comparing the Dwight Building (No. 49), which
has a design of the same general character.

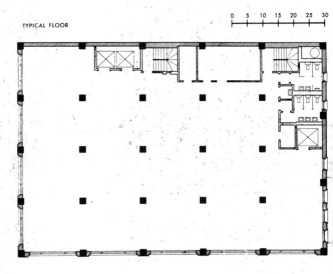

TYPICAL FLOOR

0   5   10   15   20   25   30

46 Carl Schurz High School. 1909. ◆ L

Architect: Dwight H. Perkins.
Milwaukee at Addison (3600 N). Map 1.

A dramatic composition of rising verticals in the walls, suddenly stopped by the deep overhangs of high-pitched roofs set at varying levels. A very strong string course at the top of the first floor echoes the roof line. The building is fortunate in having sufficient space around it to allow for it to be seen clearly.

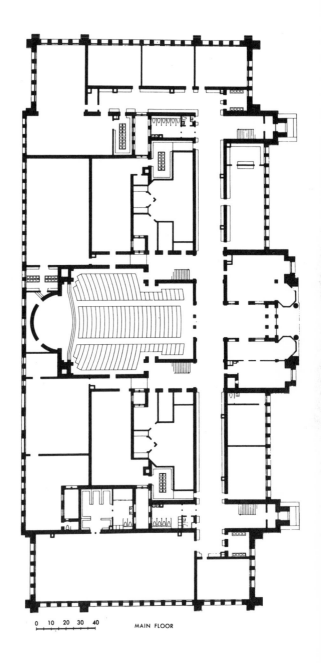

0 10 20 30 40   MAIN FLOOR

135

Architect: Frank Lloyd Wright.
5757 South Woodlawn (1200 E). Map 5.

One of the most famous houses in the world. It
shows the perfected type of the so-called prairie
house, adapted here to a narrow city lot; in its
own right it must rate as one of the most
brilliant designs in the history of architecture.
The citation by the Landmarks Commission
reads: "In recognition of the creation of the
Prairie House—a home organized around a
great hearth where interior space, under wide
sweeping roofs, opens to the outdoors. The
bold interplay of horizontal planes about the
chimney mass, and the structurally expressive
piers and windows, establish a new form of
domestic design." In 1963 the Robie House was
designated as a Registered National Historic
Landmark.

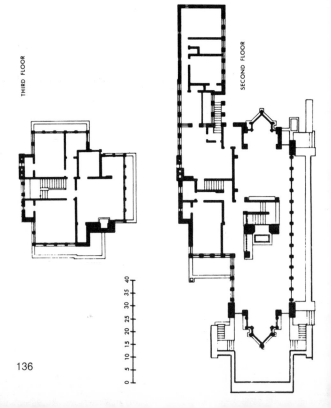

THIRD FLOOR

SECOND FLOOR

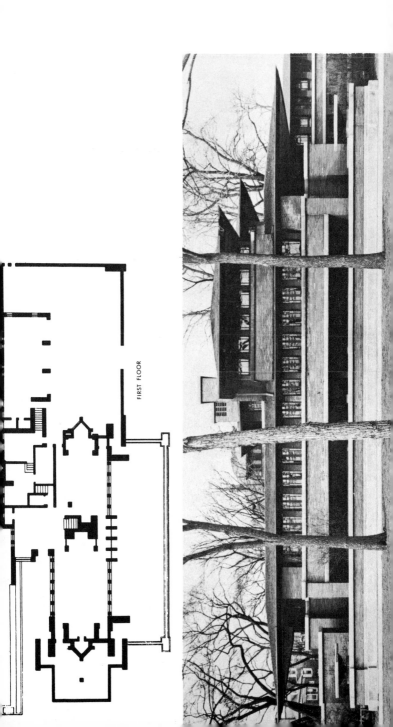

FIRST FLOOR

48 **Grover Cleveland Elementary School.** **L**
1910. ◆

Architect: Dwight H. Perkins.
350 North Albany (3100 W). Map 1.

Another example of the work of Perkins, who to
some degree specialized in school architecture.
Less varied and dramatic than his Carl Schurz
School (No. 46), it is a strong and severe
design, the chief forms emphasized by borders
of contrasting brick. The piers terminate in an
interesting capital block, which makes an
effective transition to the wall above. (By a
curious optical illusion these piers seem wider
at the second and third stories than at the first,
perhaps because of their lighter color.)

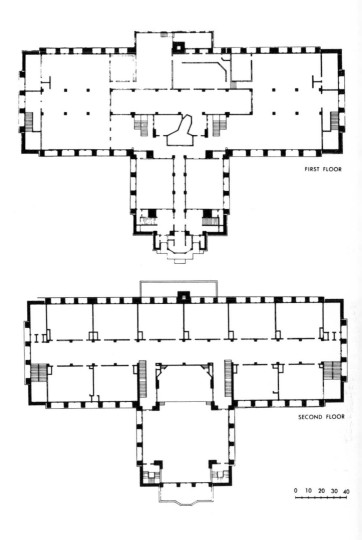

FIRST FLOOR

SECOND FLOOR

0 10 20 30 40

Architects: Schmidt, Garden and Martin.
626 South Clark (100 W). Map 3.

This building shows the application of the
general principles of design seen in the
Montgomery Ward Warehouse (No. 43) to an
office building. Similar framing strips can be
seen on the horizontals but here are limited to
the upper edge of these members. Hardly
interrupting the upward movement of the wall,
these accents distinguish the sills from the
heads of the windows and emphasize the
agreeable horizontal proportions of the
windows themselves. An instructive comparison
can be made with the Hunter Building (No. 45);
note the more decisive ending of the design at
the top and the generally greater distinction in
the proportions and divisions of the windows in
the Dwight Building.

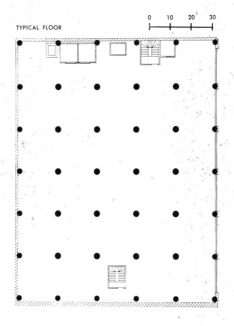

TYPICAL FLOOR

0   10   20   30

(Originally Reid, Murdock and Company.)
Architect: George C. Nimmons.
325 North LaSalle (150 W). Map 3.

This structure is typical of a number of buildings
designed by Nimmons for commercial or
manufacturing use. It is simple and
straightforward, although with some traditional
feeling, as in the massiveness emphasized at
points here. The brick is used very effectively
for its texture and pattern, finely set off by
terra-cotta accents. The building is now well
maintained and gives a good idea of the
original, although it has been remodeled, one
bay having been removed from its west side
when LaSalle Street was widened.

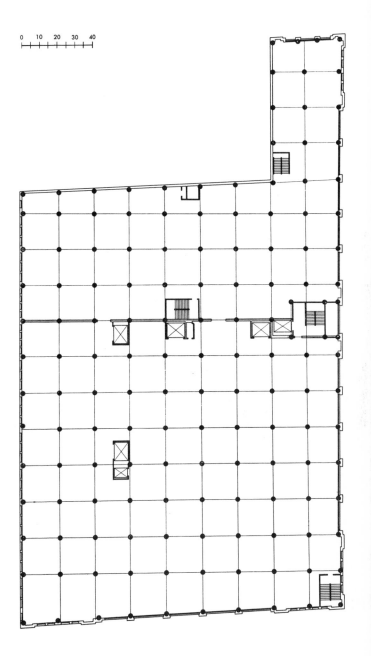

0 10 20 30 40

51 Park Buildings, Fuller Park. 1915. ◆

Architect: Edward H. Bennett.
45th and South Princeton (300 W). Map 4.

Interesting for the inventive use of concrete for
texture and pattern, as in the waffle-like areas,
or for forms inspired by classic architecture but
carried out in concrete, as in the pilasters, or
decorative strips, at the sides of the large
windows. The planning is clear and spacious:
note the enlivening of the space of the entrance
vestibule of the main building by the niches.
The links connecting the gymnasiums to the
main building have been remodeled, the roofs
of each link having had originally a small gable
echoing those on the front of the main building.

(Now the Arntzen-Coleman Company.)
Architects: Louis H. Sullivan; William C. Presto.
4611 North Lincoln (about 2300 W). Map 1.

Sullivan's last work, and still typical, in the
restrained ornament in the recess of the facade
and the sensitive patterning of the upper wall,
of his best work. On the other hand, the three
large ornamental forms up and down the center
line of the facade seem hung on rather than
integrated with the design as a whole. They
overwhelm the little facade, which is far too
short to carry such an emphatic central
emphasis.

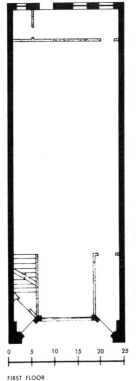

FIRST FLOOR

53 Third Unitarian Church. 1937. ◆   L

Architect: Paul Schweikher, Inc.
310 North Mayfield (5900 W). Map 1.

An interesting small church in the modern
manner, it is marked by direct and effective use
of brick, variety in the windows, and agreeable
spaciousness in the interior. It was enlarged in
1956 by the addition of the northern part, by
architect William Fyfe, an apprentice of
Schweikher at the time of the original design.

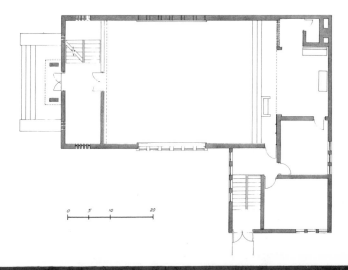

54 University Building. 1937. ◆   **L**

Architects: George F. and William Keck.
5551 South University (1144 E). Map 5.

A small apartment building in modern style. The
glass brick and the external Venetian blinds
seemed "modernistic" in 1937, but today the
dominant effect is of quiet design in simple
forms carried out in a pleasant red brick.

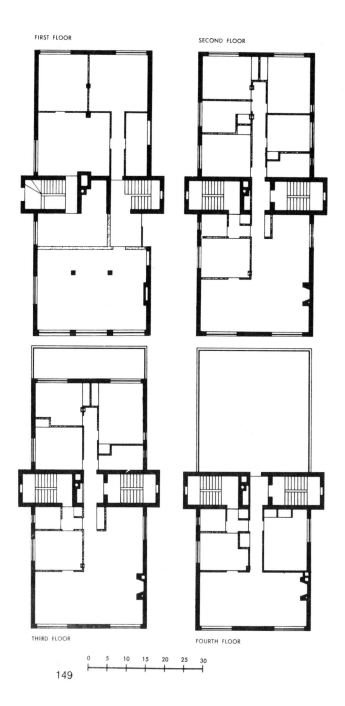

FIRST FLOOR

SECOND FLOOR

THIRD FLOOR

FOURTH FLOOR

0 5 10 15 20 25 30

149

55 Illinois Institute of Technology   **L**
Campus.   1942-58.   ◆

Architects: Mies van der Rohe; Friedman,
Alschuler and Sincere; Holabird and Root;
Pace Associates.
South State, 31st to 35th. Map 4.

Aside from the individual merit of some
buildings, the campus is of great interest for
the grouping of a number of structures by one
of the masters of modern architecture. The
buildings are related so as to suggest courts or
quadrangles, but these are never completely
closed, one such suggested space overlapping
or opening into another, usually asymmetrically.
This results in fascinating and varying visual
relationships and is highly expressive of a
modern ideal, the combination of freedom and
order. Of particular interest among the buildings
designed by Mies are the Alumni Memorial
Building, 1946 (especially for the detailing, as
at the corners); the Chapel, 1952; and Crown
Hall, 1956. The main floor of the last which
houses the Institute's department of
architecture, is a notable expression of
freedom of space.

Illinois Institute of Technology Campus

56 Promontory Apartments. 1949. ◆

Architects: Mies van der Rohe; Pace Associates; Holsman, Holsman and Klekamp.
5530 South Shore. Map 5.

This building is typical of the postwar trend toward simple style, emphasis on structure, and care in planning, for both cost and efficiency. Here light-colored brick panels and aluminum window frames are set into a reinforced concrete frame, the frame being emphasized by the projection of the columns. The columns are stepped back on the outside at the sixth, eleventh, and sixteenth stories because of the greater load on the lower parts; they are scored, but in this case at every story, in order to soften the effect of the steps by integrating them with a design element. The concrete is "self-finished," not covered with some other material, thus contributing to the simplicity and directness seen throughout.

**57   860-80 Lake Shore Drive Apartments.   L
1952.   ◆**

*Architects: Mies van der Rohe; Pace Associates;
Holsman, Holsman, Klekamp and Taylor.*
860–80 North Lake Shore. Map 2.

The citation by the Landmarks Commission
reads: "In recognition of an open plan in a
multi-story apartment building where the steel
cage becomes expressive of the potentialities
of steel and glass in architectural design."
These apartments are universally admired for
their openness and the frank expression of the
steel frame; and experts are further intrigued
by the refinement of the design, including the
subtle distribution of emphasis between the
horizontal and the vertical. Especially notable
are the small I-beams between the main
supports, which give restrained emphasis to
the vertical and also have a secondary structural
value in stiffening the glass walls that surround
each apartment. An interesting refinement is
found in the fact that the outer two windows in
each group of four are slightly narrower than
the inner two. This variation can be explained
by saying that it expresses the width of the
piers, which are wider than the mullions, or
intermediate stiffeners of the glass, and
therefore take up some of the space here. This
is an acceptable explanation, but the designer
of this facade, Mies van der Rohe, does not
always vary windows in this way. This kind of
effect is better put down simply to the creative
energy of the artist, in this particular design, at
this moment of his career, which no explanation
can quite capture. In any case, the variation
adds zest and vitality to the design and reminds
us that we are in the presence of architecture
as art rather than mere engineering, however
important the construction may have been as a
basis for the design.

Lake Shore Drive Apartments

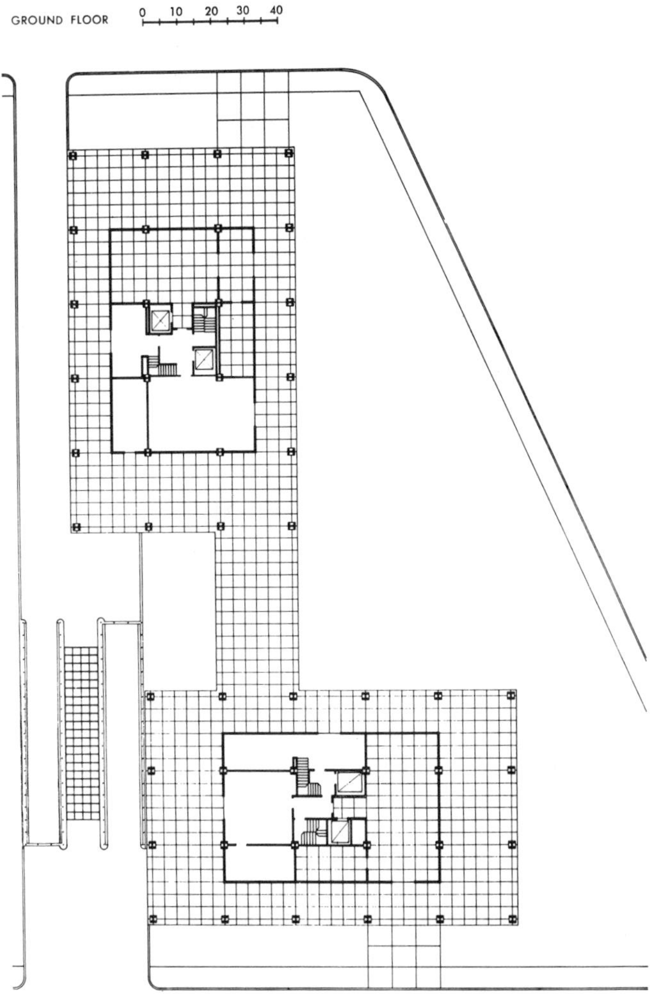

Lake Shore Drive Apartments

159

Architects: Skidmore, Owings and Merrill.
30 West Monroe (100 S). Map 3.

An interesting treatment of the "wall" of a
skyscraper, in that the columns are placed
outside the building, as it were, the lines of the
columns thus giving emphatic expression to the
vertical. The large spans possible in modern
steel construction allowed the architects to
dispense with interior columns, so that complete
freedom for the division or arrangement of the
space of each floor was achieved. The citation
by the Landmarks Commission reads: "In
recognition of the fine open relationship of the
building elements to the site; the expression of
space and structure achieving clarity and
lightness through stainless steel and glass."
The placing of the elevators and stairs in a
separate structure, to the east, contributes to
the freedom of the interior in the building proper
and lends interest to the exterior as a whole.

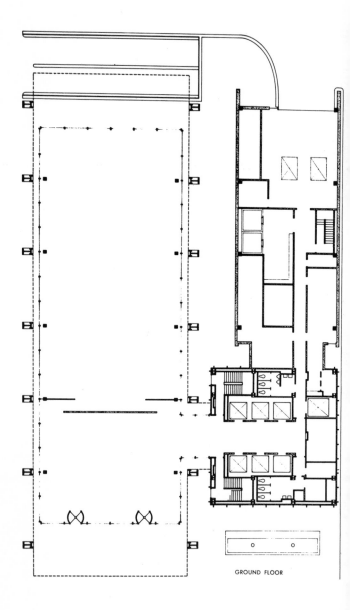

GROUND FLOOR

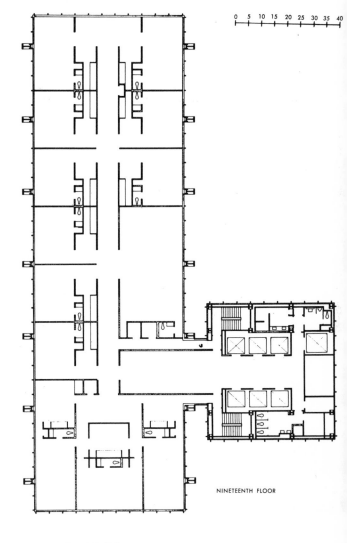

NINETEENTH FLOOR

Inland Steel Building

59 Lake Meadows. 1956-60. ◆

Architects: Skidmore, Owings and Merrill.
31st to 35th and Martin Luther King, Jr., Drive
(400 E). Map 4.

A contemporary answer to the need for housing
in a large city, in a redevelopment project
undertaken by private capital. Various types of
buildings are involved, including apartment
buildings, shopping center, school, professional
building, and recreation center, with much open
and park space provided. The apartment
buildings are in the modern manner, often with
walls of glass hung like curtains several inches
outside the supports.

60 Wright House and Studio. 1889-95. ■

Architect: Frank Lloyd Wright.
951 Chicago, Oak Park. Map 6.

Frank Lloyd Wright's house and studio, the
construction of which began in 1889 (when
Wright was but twenty-two years of age) and
continued for a period of more than six years,
provide an interesting study in form and
development.

The house, facing Forest Avenue, was built first
and is derivative of the "shingle" style of the
1880's. Wright was still in the offices of Adler
and Sullivan at that time and had not as yet
developed his own idiom. It is interesting to
note that Wright used several pieces of the
ornamental castings from Adler and Sullivan's
Auditorium building in the ceiling of his living
room. The Auditorium was under construction
at the same time.

The studio, however, was built after Wright had established his own practice; and although it is connected to the house, it is a separate entity. The design anticipates Wright's work in the years after the turn of the century. The plan is a precursor of the open plans of the later years, and the use of materials reflects Wright's thinking of that period.

The octagonal library was the last element added to the complex, which also includes a second-story, barrel-vaulted playroom, added in 1893. Alterations have been made to the house and studio to accommodate several apartments, although the studio has been partially restored and opened to the public in recent years.

61 Winslow House. 1893. ■

Architect: Frank Lloyd Wright.
515 Auvergne, River Forest. Map 6.

The William H. Winslow house was Frank Lloyd
Wright's first independent commission.

The house is highly reminiscent of the work of
Louis Sullivan, particularly in the exterior,
second-story frieze and in the fenestration. The
planning is, for Wright, extremely formal and
reflects a conservative attitude which the young
architect had at this time.

This house has been well maintained and
remains in excellent condition. The stable, or
garage, to the rear of the house was built at the
same time and is more of an anticipation of
Wright's later style.

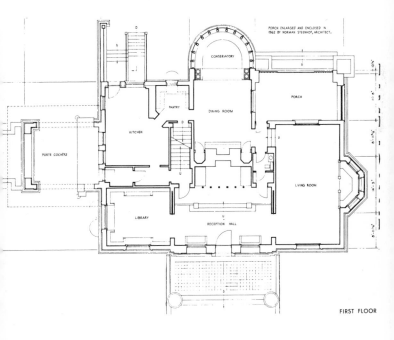

PORCH ENLARGED AND ENCLOSED IN
1962 BY NORMAN STEENHOF, ARCHITECT.

CONSERVATORY

PANTRY

DINING ROOM

PORCH

KITCHEN

PORTE COCHÈRE

LIVING ROOM

LIBRARY

RECEPTION HALL

FIRST FLOOR

171

62 Willits House. 1902. ■

Architect: Frank Lloyd Wright.
1145 Sheridan, Highland Park. Map 1.

One of the earliest and most successful of the large prairie houses was the Ward W. Willits house, built in 1902. The cruciform plan is basic to literally dozens of houses that followed, designed by Wright and also by members of his school.

A huge multiple fireplace forms the core of the design with the remainder of the house surrounding it. The major rooms have windows on three sides, and circulation is extraordinarily well planned. Sleeping rooms on the second floor are similarly grouped around the central fireplace core. In recent years the house has been slightly remodeled on the interior, although the exterior is in very nearly original condition. A gardener's cottage on the same site, also by Wright, has been remodeled as a separate residence.

63 Brown House. 1905. ■

Architect: Frank Lloyd Wright.
2420 Harrison, Evanston. Map 1.

Throughout his life Frank Lloyd Wright was interested in the problem of low-cost housing for the middle-class family. He was never able to exercise his talent in this area to any great degree. Perhaps the nearest he came to solving the problem was in the Evanston model home built for Charles E. Brown in 1905.

This house is essentially the so-called four square house that was developed from a design done for *The Ladies Home Journal* in 1901. Sometimes referred to as an economy prairie house, this design and others like it were quite successful solutions to the small economical house problem. The Evanston model home was to serve as the first of a community of similar houses, but the project was never carried out.

64 Glasner House.   1905. ■

Architect: Frank Lloyd Wright.
850 Sheridan, Glencoe. Map 1.

This interesting house with its horizontal
board-and-batten siding was designed by
Wright in 1904 and built in the following year.
It has an unsymmetrical plan around a long
central axis with the primary living areas on the
top floor. The lower level contains bedrooms as
well as a large studio and a garage.

The site, on the edge of a deep ravine, is
heavily overgrown with vegetation, obscuring
the view except during the winter months. The
present owner restored the house to its original
condition in 1926 and has maintained it since
that time.

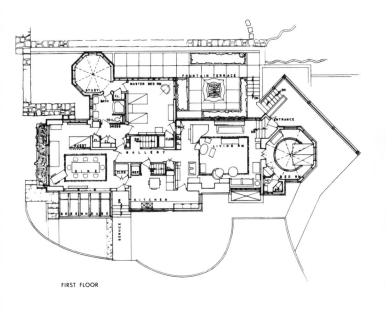

FIRST FLOOR

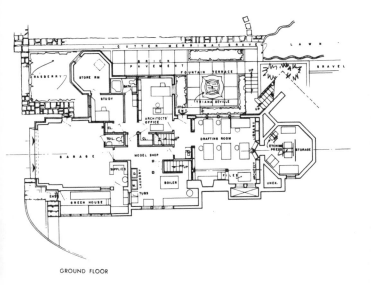

GROUND FLOOR

175

65 Unitarian Universalist Church and Parish House. (Unity Temple.) 1906. ■

Architect: Frank Lloyd Wright.
Lake at Kenilworth, Oak Park. Map 6.

This monolithic concrete structure was Wright's solution to a problem presented by the low budget of the small Unitarian congregation of Oak Park, Illinois. Wright had used concrete previously in the E-Z Polish Factory in Chicago, and had suggested its use as early as 1894 when his first "Concrete Monolithic Bank" was designed.

Unity Temple is actually two spaces, Unity Church and a parish house, connected by a low link which serves as an entrance. Both main buildings are lighted by high wall windows or skylights featuring some of Wright's finest abstract glass designs. The auditorium is a cube with the pulpit set well into the space, giving a sense of closeness between the speaker and the parishioners.

The parish house is a small cube with wings extending from two sides to provide for classrooms and meeting spaces. In recent years the building has been refurbished and minor changes have been incorporated in the parish house; however, it is essentially unchanged from Wright's original design.

The ornamental concrete work of the exterior piers is repeated on each facade. This was accomplished in an economical and logical fashion through reuse of the carefully constructed wooden molds for each of six major walls. These molds were designed to coordinate the massive concrete ornament with the delicate glazing of the structure.

For this period of Wright's career Unity Temple is a unique creation. No other building of similar character was completed until his California work twenty years later.

PLAN AUDITORIUM LEVEL
N   SCALE ⅛"=1'-0"
5   0'   5   10'   15'

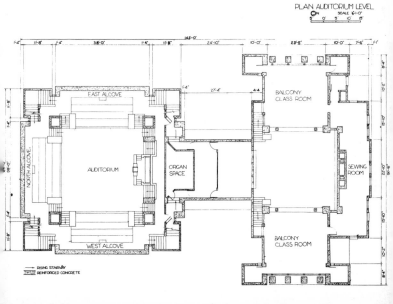

EAST ALCOVE

AUDITORIUM

ORGAN SPACE

NORTH ALCOVE

WEST ALCOVE

BALCONY CLASS ROOM

SEWING ROOM

BALCONY CLASS ROOM

RISING STAIRWAY
REINFORCED CONCRETE

66 Coonley House. 1908. ■

Architect: Frank Lloyd Wright.
300 Scottswood, Riverside. Map 6.

The Avery Coonley house is in a class that
includes only the very best of Frank Lloyd
Wright's work—the Frederick C. Robie house
and Unity Temple are perhaps the other prime
examples in this category.

The Coonley house, in itself a large building, is
but a part of an extensive complex which
included a gardener's cottage, a garage
building, formal gardens, a pool, a service
court, and excellent landscaping throughout.

The house is designed with most of the principal rooms on a second level over a raised ground floor. The massing is extremely complex but forms a unified whole with nearly every portion liberally sprinkled with "Wrightian" ornament. The color scheme is dominated by earthen hues; but bits of brilliant red, green, and gold are used for emphasis throughout the house.

The grounds of the Coonley estate no longer exist in their original extent, having been largely disposed of for construction of new houses. Thus, the house now suffers from crowding by its neighbors.

67 Drummond House. 1909. ■

Architect: William Drummond.
559 Edgewood, River Forest. Map 6.

William Drummond, practicing both alone and with his partner, Louis Guenzel, was one of the most successful of the many persons trained by Frank Lloyd Wright in his Oak Park Studio. In refining Wright's concept of the economical prairie house in the design of his own house, he achieved an architectural gem.

The plan of the first floor is almost completely open with only the kitchen separated. The second floor is done in a conventional manner. Throughout, the house is furnished with pieces designed by Drummond, which contribute to the effect of livability.

68 Mrs. Thomas H. Gale House. 1909. ∎

Architect: Frank Lloyd Wright.
6 Elizabeth, Oak Park. Map 6.

The house Frank Lloyd Wright designed for
Mrs. Thomas H. Gale in 1909 remains as one
of his most successful essays in small house
design. The cantilevers, interlocking forms, and
voids—each tied to the central fireplace core
—all combine to demonstrate the ability of
Wright to integrate simple shapes into a
complex but superb whole. To some authorities
it anticipates the spirit and character of the
International style that was to develop in the
next three decades.

The building has recently been meticulously
restored by its present owner. In its present
condition this house can be favorably compared
to any other of Wright's works, but it is most
often considered as a companion to
Fallingwater, built a quarter of a century later.

69 Carter House. 1910. ∎

Architect: Walter Burley Griffin.
1024 Judson, Evanston. Map 1.

Walter Burley Griffin worked in the Oak Park
Studio of Frank Lloyd Wright for approximately
five years. He established his own practice in
1907, after which he did a number of
outstanding residences in Chicago and vicinity.

For several years Griffin's style was very similar
to Wright's, but later his work showed more
individuality. This house for Frederick B.
Carter, Jr., which was built in 1910, is
reminiscent of Wright; but Griffin's signature
is beginning to be seen in the heavier design
elements and in the use of both brick and
stucco, a combination Wright seldom employed.
This house, like most of Griffin's designs, has
the added advantage of a site completely
landscaped by the architect. Griffin was an
early advocate of professional landscape
design, as well as an accomplished city
planner.

70 Lewis House. 1940. ■

Architect: Frank Lloyd Wright.
Little St. Mary's Road, Libertyville. Map 1.

Of the seventy-five or more buildings designed
by Frank Lloyd Wright in Chicago and its
suburbs, less than ten were built after 1910.
One of the latter was the house for Lloyd Lewis
on the Des Plaines River near Libertyville, done
in 1940. It is an excellent example of Wright's
Usonian period of small house design.

The house is constructed of Chicago common
brick and cyprus. The wood on the exterior has
been permitted to weather to a lovely silver
gray color. The interior woodwork was waxed
without further finishing. The result is an
extraordinary demonstration of what Wright was
able to do with his materials.

The house is designed so that the foundation rises above the site to afford protection from possible overflow of the Des Plaines River; thus all rooms are high enough to provide a fine view of the surrounding flat, wooded terrain. The plan is strictly in accordance with the basic plan that Wright used for so many of his Usonian houses during the last quarter century of his life.

IV Buildings of General Interest

71 Henry B. Clarke House.   1836.   ▲

Architect unknown.
4526 South Wabash (45 E). Map 4.

Sometimes known as the Widow Clarke House, this is the oldest building still standing in Chicago, although it has been moved from its original site near 16th Street and Michigan. Its portico, or porch, has been removed, as well as the original tall window shutters. But the proportions, the placing of the windows, and even the tower-like cupola on top, remain. The influence of classical models is seen in the low-pitched gable on the front, as well as in the simple moldings. The spaciousness of the first elegant homes of the city is suggested by the triple-sashed windows, which tell of the high-ceilinged rooms within.

72 Holy Family Church.   1860.   ▲

Architect: John M. Van Osdel?

St. Ignatius High School (College).   1869.

Architect unknown.
1076 and 1072 West Roosevelt (1200 S).
Map 1.

A great barnlike building of brick, this church
follows the Gothic style, as seen in the pointed
arches found not only over the large openings
but also as small components of the
"corbel-tables" (compare No. 1). Alternation of
windows and buttresses in the walls of the side
aisles results in a simple rhythm of some
interest; but throughout the building one is
struck most by a self-conscious and artificial
use of Gothic details, as in the combination of
a pointed arch and a gable in relief over it,
found both on the exterior and in the interior.
The facade is of painted-over brick; and the
interior piers are also of brick but covered with
stucco in imitation of stone. The smaller tower
is of stone and the larger one of sheet metal.

Various parts of the present church were built
at different dates, and several architects were
involved, of whom Van Osdel was one. He
apparently designed, or carried out from some
other architect's design, the original facade and
the main body of the church, both finished in
1860; and presumably he also executed the
transepts, finished in 1862. In 1866 the facade
was torn down and rebuilt, wider and some
distance south of its original location, in order
to enlarge the church in that direction, the
central part being rebuilt exactly as before. The
larger tower (designed by Judas Huber) was
built in 1874. The adjacent high school (college)
is considerably more attractive than the church
because of its greater simplicity and directness,
but I do not know of any evidence to show
who its architect was.

73 First Congregational Church. 1871. ▲

(Originally the Union Park Congregational Church.)
Architect: Gurdon P. Randall.
44 North Ashland (1600 W). Map 1.

This building is typical of a number of churches, built shortly before and after the Great Fire, which followed the Gothic style but in a free, sometimes inventive, manner. They were often built of the local limestone called Joliet stone or Lemont limestone (or even "Athens marble") seen in this church. A large plaque in the north wall of the tower gives the original name and dates the laying of the cornerstone as 1869. The interior is noteworthy. The shallow transepts hardly show, except in the ceiling, so that the interior becomes a single centralized space, dominated by a dramatic balcony. This begins as a continuation of the choir space behind the pulpit, then sweeps in a great circle around the auditorium, rising and becoming rapidly wider toward the back. The result is an impressive adaptation to congregational use, the minister being placed as it were in the midst of the congregation. (The structure was strengthened in 1927, but apparently without changing the architectural forms.)

74 Fine Arts Building. 1884. ▲

(Originally the Studebaker Building.)
Architect: S. S. Beman.
410 South Michigan (100 E). Map 3.

This building was long notable as a focus of
Chicago's artistic life, because of the cultural
events that took place in it and the artists who
had studios in it. As features of the architectural
composition, the two large columns in the third
and fourth stories seem incongruous in the
design, perhaps needing others to keep them
company. The search for variety in the shapes
and groupings of the windows is carried out
along the same general lines as in the
Auditorium (No. 18) next door, but the result
here suffers from comparison with that more
masterly design.

75 The Art Institute. 1892. ▲

Architects: Shepley, Rutan and Coolidge.
Michigan (100 E) at Adams (200 S). Map 3.

Chief home of the visual arts in Chicago, the
building, like many museums of its time, was
inspired by the architectural tradition of the
Renaissance, as taught in the École des Beaux
Arts in Paris, and is thus frankly traditional in
character. The McKinlock Court, built in 1924
in the eastern enlargement, Coolidge and
Hodgson architects, is a pleasant oasis of
classicism. Here lunch is served in the open
air in summer. The classical arcades of the
court are not quite overwhelmed by the rout of
sea creatures in the fountain by Carl Milles.
(This fountain, set up in 1931, is a duplicate
of one in Lidingo, Sweden.)

76 Newberry Library. 1892. ▲

Architect: Henry I. Cobb.
60 West Walton (932 N). Map 2.

Housing one of the great research collections
of the Midwest, the building was built to the
specifications of a strong-minded librarian who
insisted on such features as hallways
constructed almost as separate buildings, in
order to preserve quiet in the reading rooms.
The massive, Romanesque style follows H. H.
Richardson's example and was used by Cobb
in several other buildings of Chicago and
vicinity, such as the former home of the Chicago
Historical Society (later the Institute of Design,
now the Studio Building, 632 North Dearborn).

77 The Coliseum. 1900. ▲

Architects: Frost and Granger.
Engineers: E. C. and R. M. Shankland.
1513 South Wabash (45 E). Map 4.

A building of varied associations: the Republican National Convention met in it from 1904 to 1920; many notables of society were regularly seen here at the annual horse show, including occasional out-of-town visitors such as Alice Roosevelt and J. P. Morgan; whereas very different strata of society paraded under its great arches at the First Ward Ball, held here for many years.

The architecture itself is almost equally varied. The strange battlemented sections on Wabash Avenue are the remains of a wall built in 1889 around Libby Prison! (The prison had been removed from Richmond, Virginia, by a group of enterprising promoters and re-erected here as a Civil War memento and museum, standing on this site from 1889 until 1899.) In the present building, of 1900, the twelve great arches, three-hinged trusses in design, which cover the large area without interior supports, recall the development of construction in iron and steel of the nineteenth century. (These arches collapsed during construction, killing eleven workmen, apparently because of lack of care on the part of the construction gangs, since when re-erected they held securely.) The task of Charles S. Frost and his partner, the architects, was hardly more than to put a shell around the engineers' trusses. In doing this they were perhaps inspired by recollection of the exterior of ancient Roman vaulted buildings.

78 Wrigley Building. 1921, 1924. ▲

Architects: Graham, Anderson, Probst and White.
North Michigan (100 E) at the River (north bank). Map 3.

The first of the celebrated skyscraper group at Michigan and the River (see also Nos. 79 and 103). The terra-cotta sheathing of the frame carries rather commonplace ornament derived from Renaissance designs, and the building achieved fame through traits other than architectural merit. It was floodlit from the beginning, and because of the almost white terra-cotta, furnished visitors of the 1920's with a dazzling sight. Behind the thin screen that unites the main building and its annex is a handsome little plaza with planting and fountain nicely scaled to the narrow area.

79 Tribune Tower. 1925. ▲

Architects: Hood and Howells.
North Michigan (100 E) at the River
(north bank). Map 3.

Familiar to the general public as the home of
the *Chicago Tribune* and among architects and
students of architecture as the winning design
in an international competition held by the
Tribune in 1922. Although this Gothic revival
design won first place, the wide discussion of
the award led to general agreement that the
modern office building, or skyscraper, should
be designed in a modern style. The discussion
his obscured some of the virtues which,
modern or not, this building has, such as the
active and picturesque silhouette and the
interesting treatment of the wall, with vertical
sections of different widths. The simpler brick
structure just east of and joined to the Tower
was built as a separate building, the Tribune
Plant, and designed by architect Jarvis Hunt.
(Its south side was surfaced with stone in
1965.)

80 Riverside Plaza.   1929.   ▲

Architects: Holabird and Root.
400 West Madison. Map 3.

Originally the Chicago Daily News Building, the
Riverside Plaza was the first Chicago building
to be erected on railroad air rights, in this case
on the north track layout of the recently
completed Union Station. By placing the narrow
office block on the west edge of the site, the
architects opened half the lot area to a broad
plaza that faces the Civic Opera House on the
east side of the river. The simple slab-like form
of the steel-framed building, the vertical bands
suggesting piers or pilasters at the base, end
bays and top, the block-like masses of the
wings, and the emphatic symmetry are all
distinguishing features of the purified
skyscraper style that flourished briefly in the
late 1920's. The Riverside Plaza shows greater
variety of surface treatment than one ordinarily
finds among its counterparts in New York
and Chicago.

81 John G. Shedd Aquarium. 1929. ▲

Architects: Graham, Anderson, Probst and White.
South Lake Shore at East Roosevelt (1200 S).
Map 4.

The entrance portico of the aquarium is the gabled facade of a Doric temple. The actual plan of the main building is a Greek cross, but since the inner corners of the cross are filled in, the resulting shape is more like an octagon with blunt wings extending along the east-west and north-south lines. The central rotunda is surmounted by a low octagonal tower roofed by a pyramidal skylight. The soft diffused light that descends through this skylight onto the circular pool and vine-covered island below forms one of the pleasing features of the aquarium. The smooth exterior walls of Georgia marble sheathing are punctuated by narrow windows on the diagonal sides of the enclosures, behind which the working areas are located. The white-walled building was clearly designed to express the bright translucency of shells and coral. This quality and the simplified classical detail make it appropriate both to its sparkling lakeshore setting and to the dim aqueous luminosity of its interior.

82 Merchandise Mart. 1929-30. ▲

Architects: Graham, Anderson, Probst and White.
The River (north bank) between Wells (200 W) and Orleans (340 W). Map 3.

Notable for years (until the Pentagon was built in Washington, D.C.) as the world's largest building (in floor area about four million square feet). It is also notable as one of the sites of the ''markets'' of furniture and furnishings, attended by buyers from all over the country, in which new offerings are displayed in showrooms maintained by manufacturers. The style is ''modern'' of the 1920's.

83 Playboy Building. 1929-30. ▲

Architects: Holabird and Root.
919 North Michigan (100 E). Map 2.

One of the first skyscrapers in Chicago to
adopt the simplified modern style, it contrasts
with the Tribune (No. 79) and others treated in
historical styles. It achieves a lively silhouette
of rising masses by its use of setbacks. A
familiar sight to Chicagoans is its Lindbergh
Beacon, which serves as a guide to airplanes.

84 Max Adler Planetarium.   1930.   ▲

Architect: Ernest Grunsfeld.
East end of Achsah Bond (1300 S). Map 4.

The first planetarium building to be erected in
the United States is a design of classic
simplicity and purity. The main structure is
basically a regular 12-sided figure developed
into three concentric enclosures rising in tiers
as they contract in diameter. The innermost of
the three contains the cylindrical planetarium
chamber and is surmounted by a lead-sheathed
hemispherical dome hanging from an inner
dome which serves as a projection screen. The
main building volume is sheathed in polished
red-and-black granite, its ornamentation
reduced chiefly to narrow fluting at the corners
of the polygons. The harmony of the geometric
forms, the rich material of the exterior covering,
and the elevation of building well above the
level of the drive that encircles it give the Adler
Planetarium an elegance and dignity that are
enhanced by its very simplicity. The setting is
without parallel among American cities—the
view from the site, which lies far out in the
lake at the end of a long peninsula, includes
Chicago Harbor and behind it one of the
greatest urban vistas in the world.

85 Crow Island School. 1940. ▲

Architects: Eliel and Eero Saarinen; Perkins, Wheeler and Will.
1112 Willow, Winnetka. Map 1.

This pleasingly scaled elementary school in a spacious and leafy suburban setting was one of the first to revive a modern scholastic architecture, which was originally created by Dwight Perkins in Chicago in 1905–10. The local board of education wanted a school that would answer the emotional and intellectual needs of children and would fit their physical scale. The aim was to make the school environment as pleasant and comfortable as possible, so that it might become a positive tool in enhancing the learning process. The architects began with the design of a single classroom, a self-contained prototype that might be used with suitable variations for all age groups. The ultimate design then became a matter of multiplying these units along three wings extending from a central section devoted to common facilities. The classrooms project outward in subsidiary wings from the corridors, each pair of rooms enclosing its associated outdoor play space. The warm color and pleasant texture of brick and wood, the glazed ceramic sculpture set at intervals in the exterior walls, and the delightful scale redeem an otherwise excessively sober design.

86 Sun-Times Building. 1957. ▲

Architects: Naess and Murphy.
North Wabash (45 E) at the River (north bank).
Map 3.

A modern newspaper plant, easily accessible
to the public, where one can see the presses
in operation from the hallways. The treatment
of the exterior of the walls is of interest. The
plaza (to the east) is not only typical of the
contemporary desire to provide open spaces
for pedestrians in relation to buildings in the
city but is also a welcome attempt to take
advantage of the inherent interest of the river.

87 Hyde Park Redevelopment.   Begun 1959.   ▲

*Architects: I. M. Pei; Harry Weese;
Loewenberg and Loewenberg.*
55th and South Lake Park (1700 E), and area
to the west. Map 5.

Of interest to city planners as the largest urban
renewal project of its kind when it was begun;
for its emphasis on renewal rather than
clearance (only 20 per cent of the buildings
were to be razed); and as an experiment in
large-scale co-operation of governmental,
educational, and citizens' agencies (citizens'
block committees originated here).

The architecture is simple in style but agreeable.
One wonders, however, at the placing of the
two ten-story apartment buildings at 55th Street,
between Dorchester (1400 E) and Harper
(1550 E), in the midst of the traffic. Their
reinforced concrete is left natural, at least
above the first story, and, as a result of setting
the window glass at the inner side of the
concrete frame, the windows create a vigorous
rhythm by their close-packed ranks. The
two-story town houses, of brick, have an
effective alternation of wall and window in the
design of their fronts, and a pleasant air of
domesticity is achieved in the small semiprivate
yards or terraces at the rear. The mall, in the
shopping center to the east of these buildings,
is also worth noting. Part of it is open, part
"roofed" yet with glimpses of sky seen through
openings which also allow air to circulate. It
thus contributes to the character of pleasant
urban living which marks the entire
development.

**88 Chicago O'Hare
International Airport.   1963.   ▲**

Architects: Naess and Murphy.
Northwest Far City Limits. Map 1.

An example of the world-wide transportation
terminal of the present day: a large airport,
connected with the downtown area by a modern

high-speed artery, the John F. Kennedy (Northwest) Expressway. The large-scale planning is noteworthy, especially in the arrangement of the various terminals, the fields, hangars, maintenance areas, and levels of roadway. The spreading U-shaped supports of the latter are very handsome pieces of engineering architecture.

89 Marina City. 1964, 1967. ▲

Architects: Bertrand Goldberg Associates.
The River (north bank) between State and
Dearborn (36W). Map 3.

A tightly unified complex embracing
apartments, garages, restaurants, office
building, bank, marina, television studio, and
theater. The two sixty-story apartment towers
are of concrete construction in which the loads
are carried mainly by cylindrical cores. The
parking space is a helical slab rising
continuously through the first eighteen stories
of each tower. The pie-shaped rooms extend
into rings of semicircular balconies, which
transform the smooth cylinders into lively
repetitive patterns.

90 Federal Center. 1964 (first unit). ▲

*Architects: Mies van der Rohe; Schmidt,
Garden and Erikson; C. F. Murphy Associates;
A. Epstein and Sons.*
Dearborn from Adams to Jackson. Map 3.

The Federal Center, when completed, will
include three buildings: the U.S. Courthouse
and Office Building, a tall building of
twenty-seven stories, is the first to be built;
next will be an office building of over forty
stories; and, finally, the Post Office, which will
be a low building. A substantial amount of the
area is to be devoted to open plaza, so as to
open up a space in the center of the city, and
the three buildings have been planned in
relation to this open space. Completion of this
group is a further step in the transformation of
Dearborn Street into the locus of one of the
most remarkable architectural displays in the
modern world. There are half a dozen
masterpieces of modern design ranging in date
from the pioneer Monadnock Building (No. 21)
to the majestic Federal Center itself, which
emerges as one of the most impressive
examples of Mies van der Rohe's genius.

91 Civic Center.   1965.   ▲

Architects: C. F. Murphy Associates; Loebl,
Schlossman and Bennett; Skidmore, Owings
and Merrill.
Randolph, Washington, Dearborn, and Clark.
Map 3.

The building is thirty-one stories high,
containing courtrooms and offices, and stands
on the northern part of the block, the rest of
the block being reserved for a civic plaza at
street level. The plaza is intended to provide
for civic functions related to the city and county
governments, and for general use by the public
in the downtown area. There will be a raised
platform for ceremonies or for summertime
concerts, a pool, planting, etc. The exterior of
the building is of steel and glass, the unpainted
steel with an oxidized surface of a russet-brown
color; the detail of the exterior are designed to
minimize the weathering effects of rain and
snow.

"Chicago's Picasso," a cubistic representation
of a woman's head, enlarged from a design
given to the city by Pablo Picasso, has been
placed in the plaza just south of this building.

92 Equitable Building. 1965. ▲

Architects: Skidmore, Owings and Merrill;
Alfred Shaw, Associated.
North Michigan at the River (north bank).
Map 3.

Noteworthy for the collaboration of owners and architects in reserving a large area as a plaza, in a downtown commercial building, thus achieving an openness all too often lacking in skyscrapers that are built to the legal limit of the lot area. This building thus carries further the beginning suggested in certain private buildings (Nos. 86, 98) and realized more fully in some recent public buildings (Nos. 90, 91). The design is interesting in the way it explores the possibilities of the four-window scheme— the outer two windows narrower than the inner ones—which was used with such subtlety in the North Lake Shore Drive Apartments (No 57) Here the difference in width is more obvious, and the effect thus perhaps more dramatic. A pleasant tension arises in each group of four windows from the contrast of the central pair, which are nearly square, with the outer pair, which are clearly vertical rectangles. The horizontal strip of greenish-black marble below the windows adds very different horizontal rectangles which echo the horizontals of the floors. This interesting tension, or play of shapes, helps give the building a "presence" often lacking in contemporary buildings and aided here by the warm tonality coming from the beige color of the aluminum sheathing and the light bronze-tinted glass. The projecting verticals of the exterior not only set the larger units of the design but are also used in practical ways. For instance, the "piers" between the groups of four windows, although not structural—being merely shells set outside the structural piers—carry inside them cylindrical conduits through which hot or cold air is pumped to the offices from floors housing machinery at the top and bottom of the building.

216

93 University of Illinois.
Chicago Campus. 1965 (first units). ▲

Architects: Skidmore, Owings and Merrill;
C. F. Murphy Associates; A. Epstein and Sons.
Harrison (600 S) and Halsted (800 W). Map 1.

The campus is planned around a lecture center
and a great court. The lecture center contains
lecture halls in six buildings which share a
common roof. This roof forms the great court,
approached by elevated express walk-ways
connecting it with major campus buildings, and
containing an outdoor amphitheater. The staff
and administration building is a twenty-eight
story skyscraper, the others are lower. All are
arranged in accord with a master plan that
provides for flow of traffic within and to the
campus and that seeks not only to relate the
buildings in a coherent design but to create a
campus in harmony with its urban environment.

V Recent Buildings

94 City Parking Facility ("Bird Cage"). 1954. ★

Architects: Shaw, Metz and Dolio.
11 West Wacker (300 N). Map 3.

There is dramatic contrast between the closed, vertical center part, expressing the elevators, and the extremely open wings for the parked cars, the "cables" suggesting containment but with the greatest possible openness. The sculpture on the facade, "Chicago Rising from the Lake" by Milton Horn, was planned in relation to projections in the brick existing in the original design but omitted in the actual building. As it is, its sudden projection from the wall may well suggest the rapid emergence of Chicago from the planes of the lake and the prairie.

95 Chess Pavilion, Lincoln Park. 1956. ★

Architect: Morris Webster.
Lincoln Park, off the eastern end of North
Avenue (1600 N). Map 2.

Reinforced concrete is used here to achieve the
effect of a floating roof over a section of free
space. The tables, and the simplified sculpture
suggesting the pieces used in the game of
chess, illustrate the ideal of variety in
recreation on the lake shore in good weather.

96 Law School, University of Chicago. 1960. ★

Architect: Eero Saarinen.
1120 East 60th. Map 5.

The plan is wide-spreading and leisurely, with
spacious corridors connecting a completely
closed auditorium at the east, with lecture rooms
and lounges spreading to the west. Near the
center is the dramatic library, with gray-tinted
glass walls which advance and recede in
orderly angles, the panels of which have the
elegance of fine automobile bodies. A look at
the stairways inside is worthwhile; they have the
openness often found in modern architecture,
but the treads are more massive than usual, the
combination achieving a quite individual
character.

The abstract sculpture in the pool on the north
was made by Antoine Pevsner especially for
this building and is called "Construction in
Space in the Third and Fourth Dimensions."
The fourth dimension, time, is present only in
the changing light and shadow—as in any
static sculpture. This factor, however, is
especially effective here, because of the way
in which the curving surfaces catch the light
in varying patterns.

97 Atrium Houses. 1961. ★

Architect: Y. C. Wong.
1370 East Madison Park (5046 S). Map 5.

The ultimate in reticence. The houses are
closed up on the outside, opening to an interior
court, or "atrium." The exterior walls are of a
subdued light tan brick, without decoration or
relief, the headers at every sixth course making
a scarcely noticeable variation. There is no
cornice, only a simple beam at the top of the
wall; an extremely modest doorstep leads to
the tall simple door openings. Here the
architecture quietly but distinctly says "Private."

Hartford Insurance Building. 1961. ★

Architects: Skidmore, Owings and Merrill.
Hartford Plaza, 100 South Wacker (360 W).
Map 3.

An interesting solution in one of today's chief
areas for experiment: the treatment of the
"wall" of a skyscraper. Here the glass is hung
back deeply within a reinforced concrete frame,
providing functional advantages, such as
shading the glass area and giving easier access
for washing it. The primary value, however,
would seem to be aesthetic—the introduction
of an interesting depth into the facades, a
welcome contrast to the many recent skinlike
walls. The horizontal members of the concrete
frame are slightly curved on their undersides,
thus greatly enlivening the design. (For an
early example of the enlivening effect of curves,
see No. 21.) The concrete frame is surfaced in
light gray granite.

227

99 Continental Insurance Building. 1962. ★

Architects: C. F. Murphy Associates.
55 East Jackson (300 S). Map 3.

A good example of the general level of design
that followed the appearance of landmarks
such as the 860–80 Lake Shore Apartments
(No. 57). The wall is a clear expression of the
vertical supports and horizontal floors, and the
great width of the bays suggests the continued
development of steel construction. The building
recalls modern tendencies to reserve some
space around the actual structure, here at least
to the extent of a covered area like an extra
sidewalk.

**100 235 West Eugenie Street Apartments.
1962. ★**

Architects: Harry Weese and Associates.
235 West Eugenie (1700 N). Map 2.

This inviting little residential building is unusual
in that it combines a row of one-bedroom and
garden-studio apartments on its first two floors
with two-story town houses on the third and
fourth. The bedrooms are set back from the wall
plane along the street to provide open terraces
or decks for the houses. The tawny brick in
bearing-wall construction, the generous window
area, and the traditional residential scale
represent good modern design, while
harmonizing nicely with the Victorian
architecture of the Old Town neighborhood.

101 United States Gypsum Building. 1963. ★

Architects: The Perkins and Will Partnership.
101 South Wacker (360 W). Map 3.

The 19-story, steel-framed tower exhibits the novel feature of being turned at 45 degrees to the street lines—a simple planning device which serves to admit light equally to all four elevations, to provide four little triangular plazas on the site, and to interrupt the solid row of fronts extending to the north and south along the drive. The building is the most richly clad of all Chicago office towers. The continuous columns, lying outside the main wall planes, are sheathed in marble; the spandrels are rough-faced slabs of black slate, and the windows are composed of dark glass with a bluish-gray tint. The ceilings above the open areas around the lobby and around the utility core at the top floor are broken up into planes forming shallow dihedral angles, and the column sheathing ends in sharp-pointed finials standing clear above the roof line. The shapes of these various polyhedra were derived from the crystalline structure of calcium sulfate, the chemical name for gypsum. The contrasts of shape, color, and texture in the building's external covering are disciplined by the geometry of the underlying frame, which thus saves it from ostentatious extravagance.

Temple of North Shore Congregation Israel. 1963. ★

Architect: Minoru Yamasaki.
1185 Sheridan, Glencoe. Map 1.

The entire complex includes the temple proper, offices, facilities for social events, classrooms for the synagogue school, and the covered interconnecting passageways. The temple is the dominant structure and the chief object of architectural interest. The interior space is enclosed by means of unique structural forms which could be fully comprehended only during the construction of the building. Each one combines both column and roof slab in a single continuous element of reinforced concrete, rising from a thin stem-like form at the base and opening gradually into a broad leaf-like cantilever at the top. The two rows of these cantilevers, one on either side of the central longitudinal axis, constitute the roof of the tabernacle. The space between any pair of "stems" is filled with a thin flat slab of concrete bordered by amber glass. Each end of the tabernacle is closed by still another leaf-like form—in this case a broad slab with a central rib from which two sets of veins curve outward and downward. Unfortunately, the architect elected to cover all parts of the interior of the building with a creamy white paint that softens and blurs the tense and dynamic structural forms to the point where they nearly melt away.

103 Loop Synagogue.   1963.   ★

Architects: Loebl, Schlossman and Bennett.
16 South Clark (100 W). Map 3.

An interesting solution to the problem of a
church on a downtown city street. The interest
is concentrated on the interior: the seating
arrangements and the placing of the balcony
are so handled as to counteract the narrow
shape imposed by the city lot, and a pleasant
effect of spaciousness results. The interior is
noteworthy also for the modern stained-glass
window by American painter Abraham Rattner.
The sculpture on the exterior, "Hands of Peace"
by Israeli sculptor Henri Azaz, is not so
effective, being somewhat lost in the clutter
of the street.

104 Emmanuel Presbyterian Church. 1965. ★

Architects: Loebl, Schlossman, Bennett and Dart.
1850 South Racine (1200 W). Map 1.

This brick church is a highly expressive
example of irregular free-flowing space
designed to suggest both welcome and
protective shelter. The entrance is nearly hidden
at one corner of a little forecourt that lies next
to the belfry, which in turn stands at the narrow
end of a funnel-shaped area opening from the
street. A walkway that extends through two
turns and up a short stairway brings the
worshipper to the polygonal narthex. From here
a rather mysterious passage turns another
corner and rises on a ramp between blank
brick walls. At the end of the passage one of
these walls suddenly terminates and reveals
the fan-shaped, brick-walled sanctuary with its
sloping ceiling and hidden light sources. This
intricate geometry, evocative of complex
feelings, stands very much at odds with the
ruling rectangularity of most secular buildings.
It is typical of Edward Dart's special contribution
to Chicago architecture.

105 Sandburg Village. 1965, 1969. ★

Architects: Louis R. Solomon and John D. Cordwell.
Clark (100 W), Division (1200 N), La Salle (150 W), North (1600 N). Map 2.

This extensive redevelopment project was built in a deteriorated area of small stores, various service establishments, and low-rent apartments, in which the necessary demolition resulted in fewer than the usual dislocations associated with renewal activity because of the small number of residential units in the area. The completed project includes eight high-rise apartment towers, two of intermediate height, town houses arranged in U-shaped groups facing inner courts, artists' studios, plazas, children's play areas, and exhibition space. It is a diversified but balanced plan that aims to combine the advantages of in-town living with the pleasures of suburban spaciousness. The external design of the buildings reveals a combination of exposed concrete framing members and brick panels that is particularly pleasing in the low town houses.

106 Raymond M. Hilliard Center. 1966. ★

Architects: Bertrand Goldberg Associates.
Cermak (2200 S) at State. Map 4.

The center is a public housing group of the
Chicago Housing Authority—one that stands
radically at odds with the depressing
institutional character of most such buildings.
The two cylindrical towers were designed
exclusively for elderly people without dependent
children, while the two higher segmental
buildings are reserved for families. The
structural system is something like that of
Marina City (No. 89) turned inside out: the
external walls and the radial partitions are solid
bearing elements penetrated only by doors and
windows. The fluted form of the outside walls
increases their rigidity against both vertical and
horizontal forces. The radial-circular motif is
carried out in the sectorial shapes of the rooms,
the rounded corners, and the oval windows.
Caged open galleries and emergency stairways
on the segmental buildings, brightly colored
doors, and enclosed lobbies are other details
that help to lift the group well above the dreary
run of low-income housing. The site includes
an amphitheater, play space, and a large
social center.

107 **Lutheran School of Theology. 1967.** ★

Architects: The Perkins and Will Partnership.
55th at Greenwood (1100 E). Map 5.

The three buildings that comprise the school
are joined at their inner corners and arranged
in a U-shaped plan with a landscaped court in
the enclosed area. The novel structural system
is exploited for maximum aesthetic effect: the
two-story upper part of any one block, housing
classrooms and offices, is lifted a full story
above ground by four squat piers that carry the
massive supporting girders. The light metal
framework of mullions and spandrel panels
combined with extensive cantilevers makes
the main enclosures appear to be lightly poised
on their sturdy underpinnings. The steel rocker
bearings at the top of the piers heighten
this visual effect.

South Commons.   1967 et seq.   ★

*Architects: Ezra Gordon and Jack M. Levin
and Associates; L. R. Solomon–J. D. Cordwell
Associates*
Michigan (100 E), 26th, Prairie (300 E), 31st.
Map 4.

A redevelopment project replacing a slum area
that had deteriorated beyond rehabilitation,
South Commons may offer the city the greatest
social benefit of all renewal programs because
it aims at economic as well as racial integration.
The complex includes high-rise apartment
towers, low-rise apartment walk-ups, town
houses, and a variety of community and service
facilities. Apartment rents and sale prices of
houses extend from near public-housing levels
on through the middle-income range. The
project thus acts as a kind of neighborhood
bridge between the many public housing groups
south of the site along State and Prairie
avenues and the high-rent apartment towers
rising to the north along Michigan Avenue. The
nicely balanced site plan with its discreetly
scattered parking areas and its extensive play
spaces was selected from among a number of
alternatives by a panel of architects under the
chairmanship of Edward Dart. The high-rise
buildings reveal strongly articulated walls of
concrete and glass—the lower an attractive
combination of exposed concrete with red-brick
panels.

109 Lake Point Tower. 1968. ★

Architects: Schipporeit-Heinrich Associates;
Graham, Anderson, Probst and White.
East Grand (530 N), east of North Lake Shore.
Map 1.

The astonishing tower that rises near the base
of Navy Pier is first of all a structural
masterpiece; its 645-foot height made it the
highest reinforced concrete building in the
world at the time of its completion, and its
flat-slab frame with a shear-wall core in the
shape of a triangular prism constitutes a unique
structural system in kind and size. The
three-lobed shape of the tower was derived
from a celebrated skyscraper project that Mies
van der Rohe proposed for Berlin in 1921. The
young architects who created the Lake Point
design were students of Mies at IIT and
members of his office staff, and they were the
first to adapt the Berlin concept to an executed
building. The curving form allowed greater
freedom in apartment planning and offered less
resistance to direct wind loads than the
conventional rectangular prism. The visual
impact of these vast, hollowed and swelling
shapes is unparalleled in the building art. The
curtain walls of bronze-tinted glass set in a
framework of bronze-anodized aluminum
produce reflection patterns of vertical ribbons,
ranging in color from intense golden sunlight to
deep bronze-black shadows. The two-story
base structure extending westward from the
tower contains the usual public spaces topped
by a landscaped park with a lagoon and a
swimming pool.

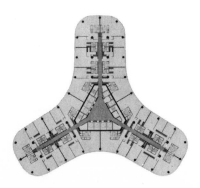

110

First National Bank Building.   1969.   ★

Architects: C. F. Murphy Associates; The Perkins and Will Partnership.
Madison, between Dearborn (36 W) and Clark (100 W). Map 3.

This gigantic building, 850 feet high, with its associated two-level plaza occupies the entire block that lies at the geometric center of the Loop. The most conspicuous feature of the visible structure is the inward-sweeping curve of the columns that stand outside the long elevations, reminding us for good reason of the Eiffel Tower. The choice of the shape arises from sound functional planning and provides us with a revealing illustration of the union of structural, utilitarian, and aesthetic elements in contemporary building design. The maximum floor area is required at the street and mezzanine levels, where commercial banking facilities and savings departments must serve the heaviest public traffic. Above the base other banking activities dictated a smaller but still extensive floor area. The space above, which is rented to tenants, meets their needs for perimeter offices and less floor area. At the very top of the building a longitudinal row of separate penthouses encloses various mechanical and electrical utilities. Elevator shafts, stairs, main ducts, and pipes are housed in utility cores placed at both ends of the building to allow maximum open banking space.

This hierarchical arrangement of functions, as one of the designing architects called it, compelled a marked deviation from the standard prismatic form of the skyscraper. A tapering envelope would provide maximum resistance to the horizontal forces of wind, but an upward-curving one would preserve the structural and functional validity while achieving the most graceful form. A somewhat parallel reasoning underlay Eiffel's design for his celebrated tower in Paris. The steel framing members of the bank building are sheathed in

gray-speckled granite, harmonizing nicely with the bronze-tinted glass. The powerfully articulated walls stand squarely in the Chicago tradition. All the visible elements in the First National Building—the curving external columns, the cellular pattern of the main elevations, the utility wings at the ends of the main block—together express functional requirement and structural solution in a strongly unified design.

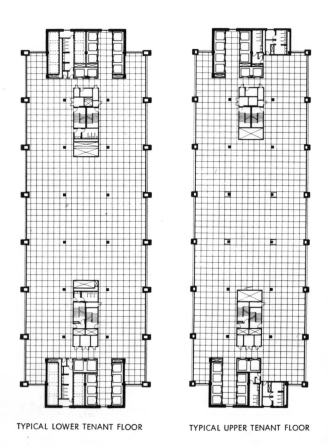

TYPICAL LOWER TENANT FLOOR   TYPICAL UPPER TENANT FLOOR

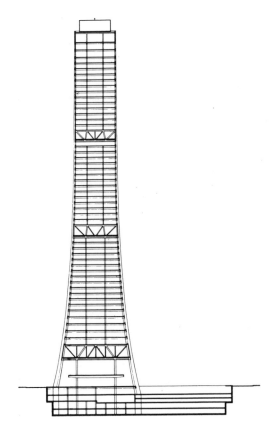

First National Bank

John Hancock Center. 1969. ★

Architects: Skidmore, Owings and Merrill.
Michigan (100 E), between Chestnut (860 N)
and Delaware (900 N). Map 2.

The 1,105-foot height of the Hancock made it
at the time of completion the second highest
building in the United States. Like Marina City,
it is a megastructure or microcity that embraces
a great variety of functions: restaurant, shops,
bank, and skating rink at the concourse level;
small shops and parking areas on the lower
floors; 29 floors of office space; mechanical
and electrical equipment, specialty shops,
service facilities, and a swimming pool at
mid-height; 48 floors of apartments; observatory,
two-level restaurant, utilities, television and
radio stations on the remaining seven floors.
The building is to a certain extent a
straightforward work of steel framing, the
vigorously articulated walls of which place it in
the mainstream of Chicago architecture. But
there are several conspicuous features that
make the immense structure a unique
skyscraper design. The tapering form, in which
all four walls are inclined inward from the
vertical, was used only once before in the
design of an office building—and then merely
to create a sensation. In the case of the
Hancock, the form was adopted to provide
maximum floor area for the public shopping
areas at the base, less extensive but still a large
floor area at the office levels, and the smallest
area for the largest apartments—thus insuring
an outside exposure for all rooms. And by
placing the maximum horizontal dimensions at
the base and allowing them to diminish steadily
toward the top, the engineering designers
provided greater stability against wind loads
than is offered by the standard prismatic form.
The external diagonal braces, each pair
extending across 18 floors, are derived from
the braced steel supporting towers for bridges
and have no historic precedent in multistory
buildings. Their function is to make the
Hancock tower rigid against wind loads, which
is usually accomplished by making all the
joints of the entire frame rigid against twisting
and bending forces. The solution for the

Hancock, however, proved to offer the greatest economy by substantially reducing the quality of steel required.

The design of the building would seem to have been dictated entirely by functional and structural necessity; yet the structural choices themselves contained an inherent aesthetic potential that the architects effectively exploited. The tapering profile is more graceful and soaring than the prismatic; but paradoxically enough, it also gives the impression of maximum stability. The diagonals add visual interest to the rectangular pattern of columns and girders by establishing a separate but harmonious geometry that serves to lead the eye from the human scale of the individual windows to the vast technological scale of the whole structure.

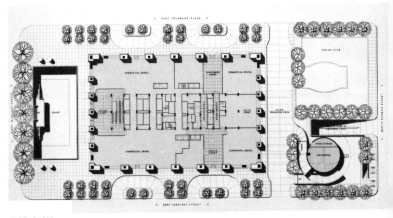

SITE PLAN

TYPICAL FLOOR PLAN

0 5 10   20

Architects: C. F. Murphy Associates
South Lake Shore at 23d. Map 4.

The first metropolitan exposition building, named
McCormick Place after Robert R. McCormick of
the *Chicago Tribune,* was destroyed by fire on
January 16, 1967. This is an architect's drawing
of its replacement, which was designed and
redesigned several times before an adequate
solution was found, represents an enormous
architectural improvement over the original,
although its setting in a lakefront recreational
area is seriously questionable. The problem
was to produce a building with greatly
expanded floor space that could be erected
on the foundations of its predecessor. The
solution was to introduce a two-level exposition
area in the north portion of the enclosure, a
5,000-seat theater in the south, and a broad
pedestrian mall between the two, the entire
complex placed under a single roof measuring
19 acres in area. The roof is carried on a
two-way system of deep trusses supported in
turn by four rows of columns spaced 150 feet
on centers. The roof is cantilevered on all four
sides beyond the walls of the enclosed areas.
The uninterrupted planes of glass extending
from the main floor level to the underside of
the roof frame and the exposed trusswork
combine qualities of lightness and delicacy
with immense horizontal dimensions. It is a
fine example of the elegance and strength of
steel construction.

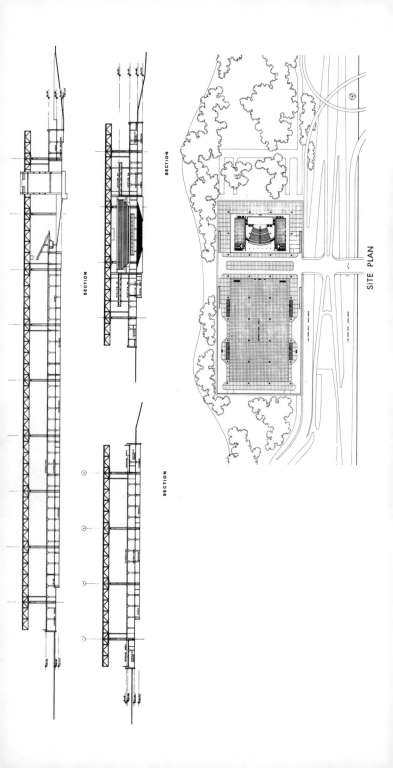

SECTION

SECTION

SECTION

SITE PLAN

Other Notable Buildings in the Metropolitan Area

Given the richness of the metropolitan area in architecture, considerations of space have necessarily limited the number of buildings which could be described and illustrated in the Guide. The following supplementary list, prepared by Professor Carl Condit of Northwestern University, is offered for those users of the Guide who wish to know the name, location, date of completion, and other primary facts about an additional selection of buildings in the area which are easily accessible, at least by automobile, and are distinguished for aesthetic or other reasons:

Buildings of Architectural Merit: The Chicago School and the Prairie School

Revell Building, 131 S. Wabash. 1883. Adler and Sullivan.

Troescher Building, 15 S. Wacker. 1884. Adler and Sullivan.

Dearborn Station Train Shed, 47 W. Polk. 1885. Cyrus L. W. Eidlitz.

Unity Building. 127 N. Dearborn. 1892. Clinton J. Warren.

Railway Exchange, 80 E. Jackson. 1904. D. H. Burnham and Co.

Mandel Brothers Annex, Northwest corner Wabash and Madison. 1905. Holabird and Roche.

Kenilworth Club, Kenilworth Avenue, Kenilworth. 1906. George W. Maher.

Evans House, 9914 Longwood Drive. 1908. Frank Lloyd Wright.

Coonley Playhouse, 350 Fairbanks Road, Riverside. 1908. Frank Lloyd Wright.

Roberts House, 603 Edgewood Place, River Forest. 1908. Frank Lloyd Wright .

Baker House, 507 Lake Avenue, Wilmette. 1909. Frank Lloyd Wright.

325 W. Jackson Blvd. 1911. Holabird and Roche.

Comstock House, first, 1416 Church Street, Evanston. 1912. Walter Burley Griffin.

Sears School, 542 Abbottsford Road, Kenilworth. 1912. George W. Maher.

Bersbach House, 1120 Michigan, Wilmette. 1914. John S. Van Bergen.

Bach House, 7415 Sheridan Road. 1915. Frank Lloyd Wright.

Immaculata High School, 640 W. Irving Park Road. 1922. Barry Byrne.

Recent Buildings: Eclectic Period

1130 N. Lake Shore Drive Apartments. 1910. Howard Van Doren Shaw.

Chicago & Northwestern Railway Station, 500 W. Madison. 1911. Frost and Granger.

Pennsylvania Railroad Freight Station, 323 W. Polk. 1918. Price and McLanahan.

Field Museum, South Lake Shore Drive at Roosevelt. 1920. Graham, Burnham and Co.; Graham, Anderson, Probst and White.

Stone Container Building, 360 N. Michigan. 1923. A. S. Alschuler.

Union Station, South Canal between Adams and Jackson. 1925. Graham, Burnham & Co.; Graham, Anderson, Probst and White.

North American Life Building, 35 E. Wacker Drive. 1926. Giaver and Dinkelberg.

333 N. Michigan. 1928. Holabird and Root.

Carbide & Carbon Building, 230 N. Michigan. 1929. Burnham Brothers.

Board of Trade Building, West Jackson at LaSalle. 1930. Holabird and Root.

Field Building, 135 S. LaSalle. 1934. Graham, Anderson, Probst and White.

Recent Buildings: Post-World War II

4912 S. Woodlawn House. 1947. Ralph Rapson and John van der Meulen.

United Protestant Church, 10 Hemlock, Park Forest. 1952. Paul Schweikher.

227 E. Walton Apartments. 1955. Harry Weese and Associates.

Prudential Building, Randolph Drive and Stetson. 1955. Naess and Murphy.

900 Esplanade Apartments, 900 N. Lake Shore. 1958. Mies Van der Rohe; Pace Associates.

5617 S. Kenwood House. 1958. Harry Weese & Associates.

International Minerals & Chemical Corporation, group, 5401 Old Orchard, Skokie. 1958. Perkins and Will.

State Bank of Clearing, 5235 W. 63d. 1958. Harry Weese and Associates.

Northeastern Illinois State College, Bryn Mawr & St. Louis. 1961. Perkins & Will.

United Air Lines Group, Algonquin & Linneman Roads, Elk Grove Township. 1961, 1967. Skidmore, Owings & Merrill.

Astor Tower, 1300 N. Astor. 1962. Bertrand Goldberg Associates.

Home Federal Savings & Loan Building, 201 S. State. 1962. Skidmore, Owings and Merrill.

Edens Theater, 303 Skokie Highway, Northbrook. 1963. Perkins and Will.

Illinois Visually Handicapped Institute, 1151 S. Wood. 1964. Harry Weese and Associates.

United Parcel Service Distribution Center, 1400 S. Jefferson. 1964. Loebl, Schlossman, Bennett and Dart.

Brunswick Building, 69 E. Washington. 1965. Skidmore, Owings and Merrill.

Dart House, 66 Dundee Road, Barrington. 1965. Edward Dart.

De Witt Apartments, 260 E. Chestnut. 1965. Skidmore, Owings and Merrill.

Gateway Center I & II, South Riverside Plaza between Madison & Adams. 1965, 1967. Skidmore, Owings and Merrill.

Holy Apostles Church, 2001 S. 15th, Westchester. 1965. Loebl, Schlossman, Bennett and Dart.

School of Social Service Administration, University of Chicago, 969 E. 60th. 1965, Mies Van der Rohe.

Chicago Theological Seminary Faculty Houses, 58th and Dorchester. 1966. Loebl, Schlossman, Bennett and Dart.

The Common, 52d and Kimbark. 1966. Ezra Gordon and Jack M. Levin, Associates.

Connecticut Mutual Life Insurance Building, 33 N. Dearborn. 1966. Skidmore, Owings and Merrill.

Scott, Foresman & Co., 1900 E. Lake Avenue, Glenview. 1966. Perkins and Will.

John Fewkes Tower, 838 N. Dearborn. 1967. Harry Weese and Associates.

Jones Commercial High School, 606 S. State. 1967. Perkins and Will.

Lindheimer Astronomical Research Center, Northwestern University, Evanston. 1967. Skidmore, Owings and Merrill.

Mercy Hospital, 2510 S. Martin Luther King. 1967. C. F. Murphy Associates.

New Trier Township High School West, Happ, Northfield. 1967. Perkins and Will.

Abraham Lincoln Oasis, Tri-State Tollway, South Holland. 1968. David Haid.

Academic Center, De Paul University, Seminary Avenue at Fullerton. 1968. C. F. Murphy Associates.

Blue Cross-Blue Shield Building, Southwest corner Wacker & Dearborn. 1968. C. F. Murphy Associates.

George Williams College, 555 31st, Downers Grove. Phase I, 1968. Mittelbuscher and Tourtelot .

Portland Cement Association Office Building, 5420 Old Orchard Road, Skokie. 1968. Perkins and Will.

Church of Christ, Scientist, Wacker Drive and East South Water. 1969. Harry Weese and Associates.

Core and Research Library, Northwestern University, Evanston. 1969. Skidmore, Owings and Merrill.

St. Procopius Abbey, Lisle. 1969. Loebl, Schlossman, Bennett and Dart.

35th and Rhodes Apartment and Town House Group. 1969. Dubin, Dubin, Black and Moutoussamy.

Time-Life Building, Grand & Fairbanks. 1970. Harry Weese and Associates.

Bibliography

Andreas, Alfred Theodore
History of Chicago: From the Earliest Period to the Present Time. 3 vols. Chicago, 1884–86.
Useful for locations and dates of many buildings constructed before 1884. Rarely indicates architect.

Art Institute of Chicago. Burnham Library
Guide to Chicago and Midwestern Architecture, 1963.

Bach, Ira J.
Chicago on Foot. Chicago: Follet, 1969. A series of walking tours of Chicago.

Condit, Carl W.
The Chicago School of Architecture. Chicago: University of Chicago Press, 1964.
The definitive history of commercial and public building in the Chicago area, 1875–1925. An amplification of the author's earlier, less general work, *The Rise of the Skyscraper.*

Drury, John
Old Chicago Houses. Chicago: University of Chicago Press, 1941.
Information on seventy-nine houses with date, location, and a picture of each, with more information on the owners than the architecture.

Giedion, Sigfried
Space, Time and Architecture: The Growth of a New Tradition. Cambridge, Mass.: Harvard University Press, 1954.
This modern classic, the scope of which extends far beyond architecture in Chicago, is included because of the importance of its insight into nineteenth- and twentieth-century architecture and because of the excellent section on Chicago.

Gilbert, Paul, and Bryson, Charles Lee
Chicago and Its Makers. Chicago: F. Mendelsohn, 1929.
Many illustrations of buildings and street scenes.

Muschenheim, Arthur
A Guide to Chicago Architecture. Chicago, 1962.

Randall, Frank Alfred
History of the Development of Building Construction in Chicago. Urbana: University of Illinois Press, 1949. Probably the single most useful publication on building in an area slightly larger than "the Loop." Despite the occasional error, the information on locations, dates, architects and engineers, costs, construction details, and references to illustrations is invaluable.

Randall, John D.
A Guide to Significant Chicago Architecture of 1872 to 1922. Glencoe, Ill., 1958.

Tallmadge, Thomas E.
Architecture in Old Chicago. Chicago: University of Chicago Press, 1949.
Readable discourse on architecture, architects, and civic leaders.

Glossary

Caisson—An air chamber, resembling a well, driven down to firm foundation material and filled with concrete.

Cantilevered—Built with beams projected horizontally, supported by a downward force behind a fulcrum.

Capital—The element at the top of a column or of any other vertical support in a building.

Chamfered—With the edge where two surfaces meet in an exterior angle, reduced or rounded; beveled.

Chicago Window—A window occupying the full width of the bay and divided into a large fixed sash flanked by a narrow movable sash at each side.

Colonnette—A small column, often used decoratively rather than functionally for support.

Corbel—A supporting form for a wall, consisting of layers or levels of masonry or wood, beyond the wall surface.

Corbel-tables—Successive corbels supporting a superstructure or upper moldings, beneath a spire or parapet, or below the eaves.

Cornice—The projecting member at the top of a wall; often a decorative development of the eaves of the roof.

Cupola—A terminal structure, rising above a main roof.

Dentils—A series of blocklike projections forming a molding, borrowed from the Greek Ionic style.

Facade—The face or front of a building.

Festoon—A decorative garland, sculptured in relief as a loop between two points.

Gable—The upper part of a terminal wall, under the ridge of a pitched roof.

Georgian—The architectural style developed during the reigns of Queen Anne and the four Georges, 1702–1830.

Gothic—The architecture of the thirteenth, fourteenth, and fifteenth centuries, characterized by the isolation of vertical thrusts of stone masonry, and the use of pointed arches, buttresses, and stone tracery.

Helical—In the form of a helix, a curve traced by a point moving in a circle as it simultaneously moves along a straight line.

Mannerist—Elaborate, highly stylized in the manner of the sixteenth- and seventeenth-century Italian painters.

Mansard—A roof having a shape in two planes, with the lower usually the steeper.

Masonry—Construction using plaster, concrete, and the applying of stone, brick, tile, etc., with mortar.

Molding—Any interruption of the plane surface of a structure, for the purpose of effecting a transition, or for decorative effect.

Mullion—An upright division member between a series of windows or doors.

Nave—The main portion of a church or cathedral occupied by the worshippers; excluding the transepts.

Ornament—Detail applied to plain surfaces of a building, whether by sculpture, incising, painting, or any other method, for the purpose of embellishment.

Parapet—A low retaining wall at the edge of a roof, porch, or terrace.

Pier—Any upright structure used as a principal support by itself or as part of a wall.

Pilaster—An engaged pier of shallow depth.

Pile—A column driven into the ground as part of a foundation, and consisting of wood or concrete or concrete on top of wood.

Portico—An entrance porch.

Romanesque (or Norman)—Various styles of architecture, in vogue up to the twelfth century, and based on antique Roman forms.

Rosette—A circular floral motif, usually carved in stone.

Spandrel—The panel of wall between adjoining columns of a building and between the window sill above and the window head below it.

Spire—A tall tower roof, tapering up to a point.

String Course—A continuous horizontal band, plain or molded, on an exterior wall.

Stucco—Plaster for exterior walls.

Terra Cotta—Cast and fired clay bricks, usually larger and more intricately modeled than bricks.

Transept—Either of the narrow side spaces, parallel to the nave, and usually separated from it by columns, in a church of cruciform plan.

Truss—A combination of straight members arranged and connected so the stresses in the members, due to loads on the whole, are direct stresses; used for beam action over larger spans.

Usonian—Term invented by Samuel Butler as an alternative to "American," in the sense of "pertaining to the United States," and applied by Frank Lloyd Wright to small, low-cost houses that he designed during the Depression.

Vaulted—Roofed by arched masonry, or having the appearance of a roof of arched masonry.

Window-hoods—A molding or decorative course immediately above a window which projects outward slightly from the main wall plane.

Credits for Photographs

The photographs not credited below are by the editor. The numbers refer to pages.

Beitzell, Neil, 78, 109, 133, 160
Cabanban, Orlando R., 192, 237, 240, 241
Chicago Park District, 203 top
Chicago Photographers, 199
Fuerman, Henry, 172, 178, 179
Hale, Stephen, 87, 89, 93, 158
Hedrich-Blessing, 146, 147, 183, 184, 198, 201, 204, 206, 207, 215, 218, 221, 231, 243, 245, 247, 255
Jacoby, Helmut, 251
Kaufman & Fabry, 203 bottom
Lane, Gilman, 173, 174
Lazan, Stanley M., 84, 85, 145
Malloch, Roger, 134, 138
Marten, Jo Anne, 66, 67, 68, 82 bottom, 142

Moore, Dave, 71–74, 80, 82
Murphy, C. F., 208–9, 247
Nickel, Richard, 79, 81, 88, 92, 97, 106, 113, 116, 117, 118, 120, 124, 137, 152, 156, 180, 182, 228, 229, 233
Peiza, Stanley, 235 top
Phillips, Dave, 239
Scott, L., 100, 101, 102, 103, 141, 153
Swanberg, Lars H., 63, 65, 98, 99
Sween, James, 108, 211
Turner, Philip, 167, 168, 169, 170, 171, 176, 177, 181, 235 bottom
Van Riper, David, 95, 96
Willett, Mike, 91, 110, 111, 128, 129

Credits for Plans

Anderson, Duane, 83
Bennett, Richard, 139, 145
Buccola, Charles, 64, 75
Dapiran, Jack, 69
Dyba, Boris, 107
Hartnett Shaw and Associates, Inc., 244
Hemmer, Melvin, 115, 121
Historic American Building Survey, 171, 175, 177
Jensen, William, 119
John Hancock Center, 253
Loftus, Thomas, 78, 93
Lorenz, Joseph, 99, 125, 132

Manny, Carter, 249
Mass, Paul, 101, 122
Murphy, C. F., 256
Omessi, Ben, 127
Pederson, Charles, 140, 149
Perkins and Will, 248, 249
Schwartz, Ralph, 111, 143
Snead, Clark, 159, 162, 163
Soller, James, 109
Stromsland, Kenneth, 129, 136, 137
Swann, David, 89
Uthe, Ronald, 135

Index of Buildings

Index of Architects, Engineers, and Artists

270

FIREFLIES